"Then BOWA Said to SCHMIDT..."

"Then BOWA Said to SCHMIDT..."

Said to

The Best Phillies Stories Ever Told

Robert Gordon

TRIUMPH
BOOKS

Library of Congress Cataloging-in-Publication Data

Gordon, Robert
  Then Bowa said to Schmidt... : the best Phillies stories ever told / Robert Gordon.
    pages cm
  Includes bibliographical references.
  ISBN 978-1-60078-801-7
  1. Philadelphia Phillies (Baseball team)—History. 2. Philadelphia Phillies (Baseball team)—Anecdotes. I. Title.
  GV875.P45G68 2013
  796.357'640974811—dc23
                                    2012051294

This book is available in quantity at special discounts for your group or organization. For further information, contact:
  Triumph Books LLC
  814 North Franklin Street
  Chicago, Illinois 60610
  (312) 337-0747
  Fax (312) 280-5470
  www.triumphbooks.com

Printed in U.S.A.
ISBN: 978-1-60078-801-7
Design by Patricia Frey
Photos courtesy of AP Images unless otherwise indicated

To Octavius Catto, one of Philly's finest

Contents

Acknowledgments

There are numerous players, coaches, and fans I would like to acknowledge for their input over a number of decades in compiling this diverse collection. In no particular order, the list includes: Charlie Manuel, Curt Simmons. Putsy Caballero, Bobby Shantz, Art Mahaffey, Matt Stairs, Cole Hamels, Jimmy Rollins, Von Hayes, Dave Hollins, Clay Dalrymple, Mike Tollin, Curt Schilling, Randy Wolf, Ruben Amaro Jr., Ruben Amaro Sr., Bobby Wine, Chuck Bednarik, Mike Schmidt, Larry Bowa, Tug McGraw, Steve Carlton, Bob Boone, Manny Trillo, Greg Luzinski, Davey Lopes, Ron Cey, Gary Matthews, Jerry Martin, Larry Christensen, John Denny, John Kruk, J.C. Romero, Shane Victorino, Mariano Duncan, Larry Shenk, Jack Baldschun, Video Dan Stephenson, Tim McCarver, Darren Daulton, Jamie Moyer, Bill Giles, Dave Raymond, Chrissy Long, Chris Wheeler, Larry Andersen, Liz Ennis, Marty Bystrom, Ramon Aviles, Dickie Noles, Garry Maddox, Al "Mr. T" Holland, Dick Ruthven, Glen Wilson, Ed "The Guv" Rendell, Mitch Williams, Jim Fregosi, Mickey Morandini, Pete "Inky" Incaviglia, Terry Mulholland, Lenny Dykstra, and Jim Eisenreich.

I also tapped into "the vault" to extract tidbits and tales from numerous past interviews and conversations with pillars of the Phillies legacy who have passed away, including: Granny Hamner, Robin Roberts, Joe Lonnett, Ryne Duren, Richie Ashburn, Harry Kalas, Del Ennis, Jackie Donnelly, Dennis Bennett, and John Vukovich.

In particular, I give special thanks to Tom Burgoyne (the Best Friend of the Phillie Phanatic), whose unfailing good humor and impossible-to-dislike personality eases the process of arranging interviews. I also give a special tip of the hat to the late Maje McDonnell, who was undoubtedly the best source of Phillies folklore and inside information that ever existed. And finally, I thank the late, great John Callison, a guy I spent endless hours with talking Phillies baseball, past, present, and future.

Foreword

What can I say about the Philadelphia fans that anyone fortunate enough to play in front of them on a nightly basis hasn't already said? It's all good! Yes, I'm well aware that outside of Philadelphia the reputation of Philadelphia's fans isn't exactly squeaky clean. Other cities simply don't understand and appreciate Philadelphia fans. That's because Philadelphia-bashers don't live in Philadelphia. If they lived in Philly, they'd join the rest of the city and become diehard fans.

One thing I've found out and learned to appreciate in my 13 years here, is that, once you're a Phillies fan, you're a Phillies fan for life. That's what we see when we go on the road. In half the towns where the Phillies play, the Phillies seem more like the home team than the actual home team because there's more Phillies fans than home-team fans. And if Phillies fans don't outnumber the other team's, they outshout them.

I appreciate that support. So does the entire Phillies organization. It's a pleasure to play in this city, and the biggest pleasure is the Philly fans.

As a Phillie, I'm also proud to be part of a great baseball tradition. Sure, the Phillies have had more than their share of rocky years. No one can deny that because, as a great baseball player once suggested, "You can even look it up!" But you can also look up and see that the fans here never stop loving their team even in lean years. Fortunately, we haven't had too many lean seasons in Philly in recent years.

In the past half-century, the Phillies have put together some really memorable squads. The hometown fans have cheered lots of diverse talents wearing red pinstripes. They've watched lots of homegrown talents blossom, like Mike Schmidt, Larry Bowa, Greg Luzinski, Cole Hamels, Darren Daulton, Chase Utley, Ryan Howard—oh, and a guy named Jimmy Rollins, too—just to name a few. Phillies teams have enjoyed some extended periods as one of baseball's elites teams. I myself am proud to be a member of one of those groups.

There's a great Phillies tradition in this town. Some memorable pieces of that tradition are captured in *"Then Bowa Said to Schmidt..."*

So for you loyal Phillies fans, sit back and soak in some tales about Phillies' players, teams, games, and whatever—stories you probably didn't read in sports pages anywhere. The tales are told not only by Phillies players, but also by some of the behind-the-scenes guys—the guys who got the scoop straight from the players' mouths.

Yes, *"Then Bowa Said to Schmidt..."* is a real page-turner! It'll have you reminiscing and smiling and chuckling. Oh, and enjoy our upcoming season, too. I'm looking for a lot of Phillies success this year. You can bet I'll be doing my utmost day in and day out to make that success happen.

One final thing—I've got to apologize for something I just noticed that I wrote a few paragraphs back. I wrote "loyal" Phillies fans. That's redundant!

—Jimmy Rollins
December 2012

Introduction

What *did* Bowa say to Schmidt? Well, lots of things over the course of their long and storied careers as teammates and coaches. But some conversations were obviously more noteworthy than others, and you simply have to read the book to find out. The answer is definitely in here. Don't be put off by the breadth of the material. The book is a page-turner that you won't want to put down, and like much in life, the journey's more fun than the journey's end.

"Then Bowa Said to Schmidt..." is not about Bowa, nor is it about Schmidt. What Bowa said to Schmidt is but a single story buried within an abundance of others—stories, tales, reflections, and recollections about teams, players, coaches, managers, fans, announcers, and mascots that have kept Philly fanaticism alive since the 1950 Whiz Kids transformed Philadelphia after long decades of being a weak sister to the Philadelphia A's into a city fanatical about its Phillies.

In assembling these tales, I've tapped the wit and wisdom of the current corps of Phillies insiders who share their insights on the recent past. I've also consulted voices from the less-than-recent past and asked them to reconstruct the glory and gloom of their times. They speak with the candid frankness that distance and time alone allows.

Perhaps most importantly, I've gone deep into the vault to revisit and rekindle conversations and interviews I had in the past with some great voices that death has silenced—legends of the Phillies such as Richie Ashburn, Robin Roberts, Del Ennis, Maje McDonnell, Tug McGraw, and Johnny Callison. Over long years, I had several talks with these men, the very men who shaped the Phillies' legacy. To exclude their rich, pioneering experiences from this compilation and permit their reflections to go softly into the dark night of lost patrimony would be a travesty.

Throughout the book, when a speaker appears in capital letters, his or her comments stem from conversations and interviews I had with them personally for books and articles I have written over the years. Those interviews span the entirety of the modern era.

This book is brimming with humorous and amusing anecdotes. Yes, our beloved boys of summer can and will be boys. As Larry Andersen, Phillies former hurler and announcer, insisted, "You're only young once, but you can be immature forever." But those same boys can also be noble, ignoble, vulnerable, perplexing, uplifting, downtrodden, hopeful, triumphant, defeated—in short, just like you and me: limited and human. No matter what the story, this book tries to plumb and convey the human elements that underlie it. I believe that's the most interesting yet least-explored aspect of any sports yarn.

Many of these stories are interwoven with the history of a great metropolis. Philadelphia, like every city, country, family, or village that ever banded and bonded for mutual welfare, has a mottled record. At times gallant and glorious, at other times flawed and scandalous, the history of our fair city and the people who inhabit it is at all times complex, nuanced, and compelling.

To borrow a lyric from a song composed and performed by one of Philly's most talented singer-songwriters, the late great Jim Croce: "After all, it's what we've done that makes us what we are." From shameful incidents in the Jackie Robinson era through the fizzling fifties, the meltdown sixties, the oh-so-close seventies, the first-ever eighties, the beards-and-bellies nineties, to the CBP-palace new century, I have tried to show my readers a landscape laden with entertaining and sometimes provocative vignettes. It's impossible to cultivate the entire bounty of Phillies history in a single volume. But in the pages of *"Then Bowa Said to Schmidt..."* you'll at least sample a diverse and tasty crop.

chapter 1

Whiz

The Phillies are Major League Baseball's longest-running continuously named team. In 1883, they debuted in the National League, known forevermore as MLB's Senior Circuit. Despite a few feeble, risible, and abortive attempts at a name change, the Philadelphia Phillies have remained the Philadelphia Phillies since conception. No other team in professional sports can match such fealty to a city and a name. Unfortunately, no other team in MLB can match the well over 10,000 losses they have accrued from 1883 until now, either. And each of those losses was marked off against the Philadelphia Phillies unlike, for instance, the Giants, whose franchise losses can be split among the San Francisco Giants, the New York Giants, or the New York Gothams.

The Philadelphia Phillies were one of sport's most inept franchises for the first part of the twentieth century. They were overshadowed and outdrawn almost every year by the Philadelphia Athletics when both the A's and Phillies represented the City of Brotherly Love.

Given the club's horrendous record in its first seven decades, Phillies history should begin in 1950 with one of Philadelphia's most cherished sports teams, the Whiz Kids. The Whiz Kids eked out a pennant on the final day of the 1950 season. They had almost blown a substantial September lead. But their near meltdown is overwritten in the euphoria of their dramatic 4–1 final-day-of-the-season win to cop a pennant—their first since 1915. The game featured heroic performances by two of Philly's most revered athletes, Robin Roberts and Whitey Ashburn. On that historic final day of the '50 season, Roberts took the hill and notched his 20th win. Ashburn made a sensational throw to nail what would have been the winning run at the plate.

The following stories tap a few of the lesser-heard recollections of the Whiz Kid era and the hopeful years building up to that fleeting magic.

Putsy

Ralph Joseph "Putsy" Caballero's soulful face morphs into a smile. "I'm 'bout the only one left on this earth you can talk to who saw the whole Whiz Kid thing play out." Putsy is a lifelong resident of New Orleans. His expressive southern drawl rolls along like a Big Easy jazz riff.

"No one in Philly would recognize the name Ralph Caballero! But they sure as hell remember ol' Putsy," he cracked. "I can't rightly give y'all a clever reason on how 'Putsy' became my name. Everybody down here in N'Awlins has a nickname. My brother, Monroe, is 'Money.' My brother, Raymond, is 'Rainbow.' There's no special reason for any of those nicknames. There's none for mine, either. People just always called me Putsy. As far back as I remember, that's the name I answered to. And that's a pretty long way back!

"I can tell you a couple funny stories about my name—things that happened in Philadelphia. First off, Caballero is Spanish, not Italian. Philly folks back in those times didn't know a hoot about Spanish names, but down here in N'Awlins, us native folks come from a Spanish heritage from long ago. You'll find lots of Spanish and French names around here. But Philly people only knew Italian names back then. I suppose that's changed, but we're talking about the era right after the big war here. Back then, they just automatically assumed Caballero was Italian. I never told anyone I was Italian. Of course, I never denied it either, but there's a good reason why I didn't. You see, in the forties and fifties, there was this Italian guy named Sam Framo who used to own a restaurant near Shibe Park. Well, he thought I was Italian, so I used to eat there free! When I'd walk in—I was usually with Richie Ashburn because I roomed with Richie—Sam would yell, 'Paesano! Paesano!' I never did let him know I was a mix of Spanish, French, and Irish—with no Italian. If I had, he'd 'a made me pay!

Left fielder Dick Sisler (8) is about to be mobbed by players from his team's bench after he clouted a three-run homer that provided the margin of victory for their 4–1 win over the Dodgers in the 10th inning of a game at Ebbets Field in Brooklyn, New York, on October 1, 1950. *(AP Photo)*

"Here's another funny story about my name. The two Phillies play-by-play announcers, Gene Kelly and By Saam, took to shortening my name to 'Putz.' I didn't think anything of it 'til one day they came up to me with a stack of letters they received. Turns out 'Putz' means a whole different thing in Yiddish. It meant something they shouldn't have been saying on the air. Some listeners were offended, so they stopped calling me Putz right quick after that. From then on, it was nothing but Putsy."

Putsy Caballero spent his entire career from 1944–52 with the Phillies.

PUTSY: "Red Barber, an old Dodgers' announcer used to say that he was settin' in 'the catbird's seat' when he was broadcasting. Well, that's where I was as the Whiz Kids team came of age. I'm the only one who was there from the very beginning. I was already a Phillie when the young Whiz Kids like Del Ennis, Andy Seminick, Richie Ashburn, Robin Roberts, and Curt Simmons first came up.

"The rest of the league was kind of surprised that the Phillies blossomed into a powerhouse the way we did in '50. In '49, sure 'nuff, we finished in third place. That sounds good 'til you consider we ended up 16 games behind Brooklyn. The Brooklyn team had a solid reputation in 1950. No one doubted they were for real. They had themselves some talent over there: Duke Snider, Jackie Robinson, Roy Campanella, Gil Hodges. And as bad as the Phillies had been for so many years, no one really believed we could be real contenders. But in 1950, we showed the world we weren't no slouches, either. There wasn't a finer pitcher in baseball than Robin Roberts. Curt Simmons blazed a fastball as good as any pitcher I ever saw. Del Ennis had as much power as anyone in the game. Eddie Waitkus could pick 'em up at first as well as any first baseman, and no one covered as much ground as ol' Putt Putt Ashburn did in center.

"Of course, the whole Whiz Kids thing kind of unfolded real quick in '49 and '50. The years before that were nothing to write home about."

Indeed. Prior to Putsy's 1944 arrival, the Phils had finished last in 1938, '39, '40, '41, and '42. They climbed up to seventh in '43, only to plummet into the cellar once more in '44 and '45, which were Putsy's first two years as a Phillie. In '46, the Phils soared to fifth place, their highest finish since 1932 when they managed a fourth-place finish

"In '48, we finished in sixth," Putsy continued. "Some Whiz Kids came up that year like Ashburn, Ennis, Granny Hamner, Seminick, and Dick Sisler. Myself, I was already a veteran by 1948. It was my fourth big-league season. Do you know how old I was in 1948? Twenty! That's right, 20! I was our youngest starter for three straight years. I started at third base. Willie Jones took my job in 1949, but in '48 Willie was 'only'

22. He was down in the minors for seasoning. And there was ol' Putsy, 20 years old and a four-year vet holding down the third-base job.

"Baseball was a strange business during the big war. Lots of strange stuff happened. You oughta write a book about that! I came up to the majors at age 16. Yes sir, I became the youngest guy ever to play third base in the majors. And I'm still the youngest, and I'll probably always be the youngest third baseman ever. I wasn't the youngest player ever. That honor goes to Joe Nuxhall. Joe was 15 when he debuted in the majors. He was one month and 20 days shy of being sweet sixteen!

"By 1948, even though it didn't show in the standings, anyone could see something big was happening in Philadelphia. Ashburn won the Rookie of the Year Award. Ennis had won it in '46. And by '48, both those young arms—Robbie and Simmons—were on the staff for good. Curt was 19 when he came up. He was all of 21 when we won the pennant!" [Editor's Note: *The Sporting News* selected Ashburn as its Rookie of the Year in 1948 and Ennis in 1946. Ashburn finished third in the voting for the official award in 1948 behind winner Al Dark and second-place Gene Bearden.]

In 1949, the Willie Jones Seasoning Project had run its course. "Puddin' Head" Jones replaced Putsy Caballero at third for the Phils. It was perhaps the most colorful succession of nicknames since King Louis the Stammerer replaced King Charles the Bald in ninth-century France. Puddin' Head, as he was known, became an instant star, socking 19 homers as a rookie, the third highest total on the team behind Ennis and Seminick.

PUTSY: "By 1950, we had it going. We brought rookie Bob Miller up, and he started off winning eight straight. Bubba Church was another rookie who had a terrific season. We had brought Russ Meyer over from the Cubs. Russ was 'The Mad Monk.' You wanna write a good book? That's the guy to write it about! No shortage of material there! As you writers would put it, 'He was colorful.'

"But our biggest asset was Jim Konstanty who came to us from Toronto in the International League. Jim came out of nowhere and had a season like you wouldn't believe.

"Everything seemed to go our way in 1950, at least for most of the year. Then things went haywire. Bob Miller got hurt. The army called Curt Simmons up and we lost him in the rotation. I still think that we coulda beat the Yankees in that Series if Uncle Sam had allowed Curt to pitch.

"As for ol' Putsy in 1950, I spent the year gettin' splinters sittin' on the bench! Imagine that—I was 22 years old and had already lost my starting job to a rookie who was older than me! That's gotta be some kinda record. You gotta check that out for me! But I wouldn't have changed a thing about that 1950 season, except I wish we coulda squared off with the Yankees with our whole roster healthy. I think we coulda beaten them. The games we lost were so close, and if we'd 'a had Curt, it woulda been a different story.

"It's probably the strangest thing you heard in an interview, but my greatest memory in baseball came as a scrub in that wonderful year of 1950. It came in the greatest game I ever had the honor to participate in—the final game of the 1950 season against the Dodgers. What a battle! We beat those rascals 4–1 on Dick Sisler's homer.

"I didn't start, and I was only in the game for about a minute. I went in as a pinch runner for Andy Seminick after Andy singled. I wanted to do something to help the team, so I tried to steal second. Don Newcombe was pitching for the Dodgers. Newk was a big guy. It took him a while to unravel in his delivery. So I took off. But Campy [Dodgers catcher Roy Campanella] threw me out. That was it. I was in the game one minute and out the next.

"Important thing is that we went on to win. And playing just one minute in that game that won us the pennant was the biggest thrill I could ever ask for!"

Schoolboy

Maje McDonnell passed away in the middle of the 2010 baseball season. To the end, Maje continued the same routine he had followed for the better part of six decades—he showed up at the Phillies' offices every day and dove into whatever task his beloved Phils needed done.

Letter to the Editor

This letter to the editor appeared in the *Philadelphia Inquirer* in 1976:

To the Editor:

My recent induction into Baseball's Hall of Fame was given so much publicity by the radio, television, and newspapers in our city that I am writing to thank all of you for my family and myself.

Having been given the ability to throw a baseball, I am personally quite proud that I was able to translate that ability into a career, which was successful enough for me to be chosen for this high honor.

I hope the baseball fans in Philadelphia, my teammates, and the Phillies organization all feel good about the part they played in my career.

The year 1976 has been something for me! I entered Baseball's Hall of Fame, had lunch with the Queen of England, was Honorary Captain of the National League All-Star Team, and was chosen Welshman of the Year, all during the country's Bicentennial.

If the Phillies can win the World Series, I may call off 1977.

Robin Roberts,
Fort Washington

Maje was a Philly guy through and through. He graduated from St. Anne's Catholic Elementary School in Port Richmond, one of Philadelphia's proud working-class Northeast neighborhoods. Maje was one of the first people ever to receive a basketball scholarship to Villanova.

MAJE McDONNELL: "Villanova changed my scholarship while I was a student there. I started out with a basketball scholarship and they made it half-basketball and half-baseball. That left more money in the pot for each program—basketball and baseball. So I played baseball at Villanova, too, and that's how I hooked up with the Phils."

Villanova sent Maje to the mound in a '47 exhibition game against the Phils. It was Maje's senior year. The Wildcats lost 7–6, but Maje succeeded in catching the eye of Herb Pennock, the Phillies GM and former Yankees hurler who was eventually elected to the Hall of Fame.

Pennock liked the way Maje threw strikes. He intimated that the diminutive Wildcats hurler—Maje stood 5'6" on his tiptoes and weighed in at 140 lbs.—had the makings of a major league hurler. Pennock said he'd work with Maje on increasing his velocity and developing another pitch. Unfortunately, Pennock—another local guy, born in Kennett Square and nicknamed the "Knight of Kennett Square"—died in January 1948. He never had the chance to mentor Maje.

MAJE McDONNELL: "No, Mr. Pennock died and I never got my personal lessons from a future Hall of Famer. Mr. Pennock hired me in '47 as the Phils' batting practice pitcher. I started as soon as I graduated Villanova. Then the Phils made me a coach. You see, the Phillies really were Whiz Kids! That means everybody was a kid, even the coaching staff! Heck, I was 29 in 1950. You don't find too many 29-year-old coaches! By the time 1950 came around, we were 'old' guys. It was as big a thrill seeing the Phils kind of come of age before 1950 as it was to go through the 1950 season itself.

"We had some other fine ballplayers come through Philly who didn't get to taste the glory of that pennant. We had a pitcher named Schoolboy Rowe for a number of years in the forties. He was our big gun—an All-Star on poor Phillies teams. Schoolboy even picked up some MVP votes for a couple of years. Can you imagine that! On a last place team! Schoolboy had winning records about four straight years before 1950 even though he was playing on last-place teams. I'll tell you what I remember most about Schoolboy Rowe. He could really swing the bat, which made for some episodes.

"One day late in '47, our manager yanked a guy out of the game and sent Schoolboy up to pinch hit for him. Not a big deal, right? But the guy he yanked was Harry Walker, who was on his way to winning the batting title that year and, after all, Schoolboy was a pitcher! He had a higher average [.363] than Ted Williams that year. I call that impressive no matter what.

"Anyway, this particular day, somehow Harry got into a tiff with our manager, Ben Chapman. Both of them were southerners, and both were hot-tempered. Harry was from Mississippi, and Ben was born in Tennessee and then moved to Alabama. For some reason that I can't remember, Ben wanted to teach Harry a lesson, so Chapman sent Schoolboy up to pinch-hit for him. Now understand, Schoolboy could have been a position player. He might be the best-hitting pitcher besides Newk [Don Newcombe] I ever saw in 60 years of major league baseball.

"It was uncomfortable in the clubhouse for a long while after that game! Ben Chapman might have been a good player for 15 years with the Yankees and a few other clubs. But he had trouble trying to manage people, and particularly, as the whole world found out, black people."

Rowe was a big 6'4" guy who hit .263 with 18 round-trippers in a 15-year career. Schoolboy had been used in the pinch several times in his career. In 1943, his first year with the Phils, he batted .306 as a pinch-hitter and led the NL in pinch-hits and pinch-hit appearances. He even whacked a grand slam off Braves righty Al Javery, which produced a sixth-inning tie in a game the Phils went on to win 6–5 in 12 innings. It wasn't Schoolboy's first slam. Rowe hit a slam previously in 1939 when he was a Detroit Tiger. That makes Schoolboy Rowe the only pitcher ever to hit a grand slam in each league. In 1947, Schoolboy made history in the All-Star Game by pinch-hitting for pitcher Johnny Sain. The appearance made him the first player ever to appear in an All-Star Game for both leagues.

PUTSY CABALLERO: "Maje is right! That big ol' Schoolboy could flat out hit a baseball. I remember him hitting in a couple of games against the Cincinnati Reds.

"We played a doubleheader in '47 against the Reds. In the first game, we went into extra innings tied at 3–3. When we came to bat in the bottom half of the 10th, it was 12–3 Reds. Just like that! The Reds—well, it was like they caught lightning in a bottle. They didn't have a very impressive lineup. Like us, they were just a second-division club. Our pitcher, Blix Donnelly, had held them down for most of the game. Then in the 10th, Cincinnati started hitting bullets everywhere, and anything

Brothers

Another one of the Whiz Kids, Harry Walker had the nickname "the Hat" because of his nonstop fidgeting with his cap once he stepped into the batter's box. According to Putsy Caballero, "He used to go through dozens of caps every year!"

The Hat and his brother, "Dixie," flanked each other in the starting NL All-Star outfield in 1947. At the end of the season, when Harry won the batting title, he accomplished a couple of things that have never been matched. His brother, Dixie Walker of the Dodgers, had won the 1944 batting championship, so when Harry won the 1947 batting title, the Walker brothers became the only brothers in history to win batting titles. Harry the Hat Walker also became the only player ever to win an NL batting title while playing for two teams in the same season. Harry started the '47 season with the St. Louis Cardinals. He wasn't producing. His anemic .200 April-May start in St. Louis induced the Cards to trade him to the Phils in exchange for Ron Northey. Walker came to the Phils in early May. His bat gained new life, and he hit a torrid .371 for the rest of the '47 campaign as a Phil to cop the batting crown.

Harry the Hat Walker left an indelible mark in St. Louis. He was a principal in one of St. Louis'—as well as MLB's—most fabled plays.

they didn't hit hard fell in safe. They scored all those runs without a homer! That Reds club was nothing like that Big Red Machine years later, or the fifties team that had Kluszewski, Bell, and a bunch of other bombers and set a record for most homers in a season. On the '47 club, nobody even hit 20 homers.

"What happened after that game, though, I think was important in building the character of the Phillies. After we got killed in the opener, our whole squad was saying, 'What happened?' But we fought back in the second game! And it was Schoolboy who led the way. He didn't have his best stuff that day, but he battled. We all came out swinging and that included Schoolboy, who hit a homer that gave us the win.

In Game 7 of the 1946 World Series, it was Harry Walkers' double that drove in Enos Slaughter from first base to score the winning run and defeat the Boston Red Sox. That play, more than anything, sealed and certified the Slaughter legacy and provided him, a hard-nosed on-the-bubble Hall of Famer, with the oomph that hoisted him into the Hall of Fame.

As for the Walker brothers, Dixie and Harry the Hat are scions of strong baseball stock. Their dad, Ewart Gladstone "Dixie" Walker, was a four-year major league pitcher for the Washington Senators from 1909–12.

Harry the Hat lost his job in 1948 to a promising youngster named Richie Ashburn who went on to win *The Sporting News'* Rookie of the Year Award. The Phils traded the Hat to the Chicago Cubs for Bill "Swish" Nicholson. To sum up, Putt Putt took the Hat's job, so the Hat was swapped for Swish.

The season that Harry Walker enjoyed in 1947 was a bit of an outlier. Over the entirety of Harry the Hat's career, in only two seasons did his at-bats exceed 500. His lifetime batting average was an impressive .296, but he never approached the numbers he put up for the Phils in '47 when he won the batting title with a .363 average.

"It took a couple of years but we got our revenge on Cincy for that embarrassment! In '49, in a game I'll never forget at Shibe Park, we hit five homers against them in the eighth inning. Believe it or not, all those homers in one inning didn't set a record. The 1939 Giants had done the same thing. But what an inning! Andy Seminick hit two homers that inning.

"Here's what happened. When we batted in the eighth inning, we were down 3–2. Del Ennis opened the inning with a homer off Ken Raffensberger. Kenny pitched for us in the forties, and we could read him pretty well. He didn't fool Del! Andy [Seminick] was next up. He popped one out to left. Andy used to catch Raffensberger. He knew him like a book! They brought another pitcher in, and two batters later, don't you know Puddin' Head Jones—the guy who took my job—slammed one out. Next thing you know, there's Schoolboy swinging from the heels and kissing one goodbye!

"Bucky Walters was the Reds' manager. The Phils dumped Bucky as manager in the early forties, and it was killing Bucky watching all those Phillies homers! Next thing, Big Muscles Kluszewski over at first base made a bad throw to the pitcher covering first on a grounder. That brought Seminick up again, and he hit his second homer in the inning. After that game, I think everyone in baseball knew that we were cooking a special stew in Philadelphia."

Putsy didn't mention another couple nuggets from that game. That same inning, Granny Hamner also slammed a double, and Willie Jones missed his second homer of the inning by inches. And finally, Andy Seminick hit a homer earlier in the game, giving him three for the day.

Wild

Robin Roberts is probably the best-loved Phillie of all time who is not named Richie Ashburn. Ashburn wins the popularity contest owing to a 34-year broadcasting career spent entirely in Philadelphia that he tacked on to his Philly playing career.

Roberts was a workhorse. Philly fans adored his work ethic and competitive streak. Fans can still picture his flawless delivery, pinpoint control, and unflappable demeanor. Robbie once confessed to me that as a youngster he suffered wild streaks, too, but somehow those early episodes have mercifully slipped through the fickle filter of time.

ROBIN ROBERTS: "I feel I finally earned respectability in 1950. I had arrived in the bigs in 1948 and found I had a bit more to learn than I thought. I was like a lot of other green kids. How old was I in 1948? 21? Sometimes it seems like I was never 21! Becoming a big leaguer isn't a smooth process. I was no exception.

"I set high expectations for myself. I had been a star at Michigan State University. I just expected that success to continue in the big leagues.

Bob Miller on October 3, 1950, during a workout at Shibe Park in Philadelphia, where the team was preparing for the World Series against the New York Yankees. *(AP Photo/File)*

But the Phillies sent me down to Wilmington my first year. I had to pay my dues. I wasn't real happy about that, but I impressed them in Wilmington. I pitched against Trenton early in the season and struck out 18. I believe that's the most I ever struck out ever, anywhere in one game. Of course, I didn't start pitching until I got to college. I advise all youngsters to take that route. Don't pitch when you're young and your bones aren't fully formed. You'll ruin your arm. Growing up, I always played positions in the field. It paid dividends. I learned to hit that way, and I think I developed more athleticism.

"I got off to a good start at Wilmington [Roberts was 9–1 before the Phillies called him up on June 5, 1948]. I was feeling pretty good about myself, and I thought I'd just keep on winning like I had in college and at Wilmington. But I found out quickly there was a difference between the bigs and the bush leagues. I lost my first start 2–0. I don't care who you are, whether you become a Hall of Famer or just stop by the majors long enough for a cup of coffee, you never forget your first game. I lost mine. But I made a favorable showing. It took me a few innings, but I got over the butterflies. The crowd was probably less than 15,000 at Shibe Park, but to me it looked like 100,000. I lost that game to a fellow named Elmer Riddle who was a 20-game winner with Cincinnati during the war years. He was pitching for the Pirates when I faced him, and he shut us out 2–0. I got a pair of strikeouts and a pair of walks. I gave up five hits—all in all, not a bad start, except that 'not bad' never worked for me. I hated losing."

Robbie lost more than he won in his 1948 rookie season when both he and the Whiz Kids were trying to find their groove. Roberts cited some growing pains that freshman-year jitters induced—episodes that don't jibe with the Roberts legend of pinpoint control and unflappability.

ROBIN ROBERTS: "I've always been flattered that fans remember my control on the mound—control of the ball and my emotions. Believe me, in my rookie season, I had some control troubles that, fortunately, most people have forgotten. Maybe I should leave it that way and not dredge it up!

Look-Away Dixie

Fred "Dixie" Walker of the 1947 Dodgers was the brother of the Phils' center fielder Harry "the Hat" Walker. Dixie found himself—or more accurately placed himself—front and center in one of the early ugly chapters of the Jackie Robinson saga.

Baseball was in turmoil in 1947, the year the great Jackie Robinson broke baseball's color barrier. At spring training in 1947, the Dodgers announced they were bringing Robinson up from the minors. Dixie Walker wasn't going to stand for it—the "it" being, in Dixie's mind, suffering the indignity of playing on the same field with a black man. Dixie penned a letter to Dodgers president and GM Branch Rickey demanding a trade. Naturally, he didn't cite Robinson's arrival as the specific reason for the sudden request. Years later, Walker said he feared for his family and businesses in Alabama. "I didn't know if people in my town would spit on me or not for playing with a black man," he explained. Dixie was born in Villa Rica, Georgia, and he later settled comfortably in Birmingham, Alabama.

Other Dodgers followed Dixie's lead and demanded to be traded. Walker denied he was the ringleader. Branch Rickey stood his ground. Walker begrudgingly relented. He played the season as a Dodger. On the many occasions that season when Jackie Robinson's teammates shook Robinson's hand after he had a clutch hit or score, Jackie Robinson dutifully and graciously looked away from Dixie. Dixie looked away from Robinson, as well. The two developed this little unspoken ritual to avoid putting Dixie in what he considered the shameful position of having Dixie's friends back home see their neighbor willingly shake the hand of a black man.

"In July of '48, I pitched the first game of a doubleheader in Chicago. It turned into a pitching duel between a guy named Johnny Schmitz and me. We were tied 2–2 in the bottom of the ninth. First thing I did was load the bases. I don't know what happened to me after that, but I kind of came undone. I hit two guys in a row to lose the game. It's true! First I plunked Phil Cavaretta, and then on the very next pitch, I hit Andy Pafko.

"I can't make excuses except to say I was an inexperienced kid at the time. Earlier in the game, Cavaretta hit a long double against me. I might have been a little in awe of Cavaretta. I lived near Chicago in Springfield, Illinois. I grew up a Cubs fan, and Phil was a big Cubs star and a former batting champ when I was a kid. He was kind of a grizzled old vet when I got to face him. Andy Pafko was a pretty fair country hitter, too. He tagged me for a couple hits earlier in that game. So I think I was just trying to be too perfect. I aimed the ball, and I paid the price.

"I had another bout with wildness a few weeks later against the Dodgers on a really hot August day in Philly. They always said I was at my best in hot weather. I'm not so sure about that. I think I just got stronger as a season progressed. When the hot weather rolled around in July and August, I was in a strong rhythm. I thrived on work. I needed a lot of work to be sharp.

"On this particular day, Rex Barney on the Dodgers threw a one-hitter at us. And our one hit was a dying duck into center that Duke Snider almost shoe-stringed. You know what the final score was? 1–0! I lost the game—no shame in that. But it's the way I lost that hurt. A fellow named Marv Rackley on the Dodgers opened the game with a line-drive single. I think I was rattled because I wasn't warmed up sufficiently, and I had served him up a fat pitch. I got into a wild streak. I walked Gene Hermanski. Then with Duke Snider batting, I had Rackley picked off second. I had him dead to rights but threw wildly into center field. I regained my composure and struck Duke out—not an easy thing to do. I only needed one more out to get out of the inning. But I threw a wild pitch. And it *was* a wild pitch. Whenever a pitch got by Andy Seminick, it was a wild pitch. Andy was as good a backstop as I ever saw. That was it, the only run of the game. Rackley scored because of my wildness.

"I made up my mind that day that if I was going to lose a game, the other team was going to have to beat me. I was never going to hand another game to an opponent."

Robbie stayed true to that philosophy. He became one of the most accurate hurlers in history—a steady-as-a-rock staff ace who won 20 or more games for six consecutive seasons. He did thrive on work. Robbie pitched more than 300 innings in six straight seasons.

chapter 2

Whiz to Wuz

The Abominable '50s

The fall came fast after that glorious 1950 pennant. The following year, the Phils found themselves pitted not only against the Dodgers' Boys of Summer but also the Willie Mays–led New York Giants. The Phillies were quickly falling behind the competition because of their reticence to break the color barrier, which they didn't do until 1957 when they signed a 30-year-old African American named John Kennedy who spent only a brief period in the majors.

When it was obvious that the Kennedy experiment was destined for failure, on April 5 of that same season, the Phils decided to ease into integration with a hasty trade. Less than two weeks before Opening Day, they sent darling-of-the-Philadelphia-fans Elmer Valo along with a few forgettables to the Dodgers for a darker-skinned Cuban, Humberto "Chico" Fernandez. Chico became the Phils' starting shortstop. He hit a respectable .262 for a 77–77 Phillies team. People of a certain age, I'm told, remember Chico best for the chants of "Go Chico, Go" that filled Connie Mack Stadium when Chico got on base. It brought life to the series of meaningless encounters the Phils played there that season. The stats corroborate that it was a dull season. If Chico's running was the season's highlight, his 18 steals were 20 less than league-leader Willie Mays' 38 swipes. Sadly, Chico's larceny was hardly the stuff of Lou Brock or Slidin' Billy Hamilton.

Suffice it to say, the Whiz Kids devolved quickly into the Wuz Kids. In 1951, the NL's season ended with the historic "Shot Heard 'Round the World." Unfortunately for the Phils, Bobby Thomson's heroics all but effaced Dick Sisler's heroics of the previous year. *Sport Magazine* and numerous other polls and publications still pick Thomson's homer as baseball's top moment in history. The 1951 Phils sank into the second division with a 73–81 log that left them 23½ games out of the chase. Putsy Caballero with his .186 average became the regular second baseman. Only Willie Jones, who made the All-Star squad for the second and last time in his career, hit more than 20 home runs. Del Ennis suffered his worst season ever. His home run production (15) was less than half of the 31 he slammed in 1950. His RBI totals dropped from a league-leading 126 in 1950 to 73 in 1951.

But the big hurt was the pitching staff. Roberts had established himself as a top-liner. But Curt Simmons, a 17-game winner in '50, missed the entire year due to military service.

MAJE McDONNELL: "The biggest hurt was Bob Miller's injuries. Bob had great stuff. He hurt himself in 1950 carrying a suitcase. It might sound trivial, but he never recovered. He never realized the promise he showed as a rookie. He was the best pitcher on our '50 staff—and that includes Roberts—until he got hurt. He started 1950 off 8–0. Miller hung around 'til the end of the fifties, always experimenting with his delivery and new pitches. But he never found his groove and was never more than a so-so pitcher. He won two games in '51, nine less than the 11 he chipped in with in the pennant-winning year. Add those nine to the 17 wins Curt Simmons had in '50 that we lost in '51, and you can see the '51 squad was in trouble.

"But our biggest hurt after '50 was the way Jim Konstanty's pitching fell off. Jim was a quiet guy, a college guy who went to Syracuse. He and [manager] Eddie Sawyer were kind of the thinking guys who sat together over in a corner! Eddie graduated from Ithaca College. Then he went to Cornell and got a master's degree in biology. Everybody liked Eddie and Jim, but they talked about different things than the rest of us.

"Jim didn't have a great arm. He didn't have much velocity, and when he started out in baseball, he didn't have great stuff. The difference-maker was that he learned a palm ball right before he came to Philadelphia. Jim showed the rest of the staff how to throw it, but

Phillies relief pitcher Jim Konstanty in action on September 26, 1950.
(AP Photo)

nobody bothered learning it. They were all young fireballers like Robbie and Curt and Bob Miller. Guys with arms like theirs weren't interested in throwing junk pitches like a palmball. Konstanty threw a nasty slider, too, just not with much velocity. In 1950, Konstanty's palm ball flustered hitters all year long. In 1951, it didn't. Hitters caught on. After 1950, he never had success again in the NL. But he did succeed in the AL. He went over to the Yanks and had a great season. Like I said, Jim's stuff could fool hitters for a while. But once hitters caught on, he was toast. Still, not having Konstanty turning out the lights like he did in '50 killed us in '51."

In '52, powered by Curt Simmons' return from military service, the Phils climbed up to fourth place. There they remained for three of the next four seasons.

MAJE McDONNELL: "The Whiz Kids were basically intact through the mid-fifties. The only guys we lost were Dick Sisler and Eddie Waitkus. But the nucleus: Puddin' Head Jones, Granny Hamner, Whitey Ashburn, Del Ennis, Stan Lopata, Robbie, Curt, and Bob Miller were Phillies 'til almost the end of the decade.

"I hated to lose Sisler. He and I were close. We traded Dick for a terrific hitter—Smokey Burgess. That guy could out-hit any catcher I ever saw. All he did was hit line drives. Baseball people used to say you could wake Smokey up at 3:00 AM, throw him a fastball, and he'd hit a line drive. You couldn't say the same about Granny Hamner. At 3:00 AM, you'd have to find him first! But that's a different story! Anyway, Dick got hurt and his major league career was done by '54. He was sent down to the minors in '53 and never made it back to the bigs. Can you imagine that? At 32, he's washed up and sent to the minors after having been an All-Star and hitting one of baseball's most famous home runs. He's kind of a poster boy for the flop of the Whiz Kids."

In '56, while they were still fielding the nucleus of the Whiz Kids, the Phils tumbled to fifth place. Roberts slipped to 19–18—the first time in seven years he didn't win 20. In '57, Roberts' 10–22 record would have devastated the team had it not been for the Rookie of the Year Jack

Sanford and his 19–8 performance. The Phils eked out a .500 season in '57, the year Chico Fernandez became the first Phillie starter to break the color line. That season proved their last brush with…let's call it the veneer of respectability accorded to teams that are neither bona fide contenders nor totally dismissed doormats.

JOE LONNETT, Phillies catcher in the fifties: "1958 was a killer, a painful turn-around year. All that was left of the Whiz Kids was Richie [Ashburn] and Willie Jones and a very hobbled Stan Lopata. Almost everybody else was gone, and Robbie was just a shell of what he once was. Aaron, Mays, Frank Robinson, and a lot of other African American stars and superstars emerged. We didn't have anybody around here with that kind of firepower in the late fifties. Philadelphia was kind of left in the lurch. And the Whiz Kids seemed like a million years ago."

In 1958, the Phils sank into last place, to which they clung tenaciously until 1961. Unknowns, never-wuzzes, and never would-bes like John Easton, Jim Bolger, Harry Hanebrink, Tony Curry, Bobby Malkmus, Ted Lepcio, and a litany of others cavorted (if cavorting can be done clumsily) on Connie Mack's turf on their way to anonymity.

Dalton Gang

JOHN CALLISON, Phillies star right fielder in the sixties: "I remember the Dalton Gang. Wow, if people only knew! I was just a kid when I came to Philly from the White Sox. Jack Meyer, Jim Owens, and Dick Farrell were all here. I'll tell you one thing—all three had baseball talent. I always felt bad for Meyer. Things just didn't go his way. He died very young, in his mid-thirties."

Sadly, Jack Meyer had a history of heart problems. He collapsed from a heart attack as he was watching a basketball game on television. A week later, he died at Jefferson Hospital in Philadelphia, leaving behind a wife and three children. His death occurred less than six years after he tossed his last pitch as a Phillie.

JOHN CALLISON: "Everybody in baseball knew about the Dalton Gang. Other teams would come into the city and ask me where the

Showdown

Philly was briefly the epicenter of both the baseball and football universe in 1950. No one expected the Whiz Kids to win a pennant. The '49 Phils managed a third-place finish. But in '50, they had to knock off Brooklyn's Boys of Summer, who were revving up into a superpower. The Dodgers and the Stan Musial–led St. Louis Cardinals, who won the 1946 pennant and finished second the next three seasons, were conceded the top spots.

When they did win in 1950, the Phils became the darlings of base-ball—if only for a year. Philly became a team to watch, maybe even the team to beat—at least for one glorious year.

The Phillies' NFL counterparts were not viewed as upstarts. They were conceded to be the NFL's best. Their roster was chockfull of nationally known stars like Steve Van Buren, Pete Pihos, rookie Chuck Bednarik, one-eyed QB Tommy Thompson, North Catholic's H.S. (in Philadelphia) Bucko Kilroy, Alex Wojciechowicz, and others. The Eagles had won three consecutive Eastern Conference championships and two straight NFL Championships in 1948 and 1949. In those champion-ship tilts, the Birds accomplished something no other team—before or since—has done. They shut out the opposition. In the fabled Blizzard Bowl of 1948, the Eagles won 7–0. In the Rain Bowl in L.A. they prevailed 14–0.

Entering the 1950 football season, the Philadelphia Eagles were the class of football. Or so the legitimate football world believed. The Cleveland Browns begged to differ, however.

Coming into 1950, Cleveland had won four straight All-American Football Conference titles. The AAFC was a rival professional football league that folded in 1949. The primary reason for its demise was lack of competition. The Cleveland Browns dominated the league, winning the league championship every year of the AAFC's existence.

The NFL dismissed the AAFC as inferior. However, when the AAFC folded, the NFL deigned to ask a few of the stronger AAFC teams, including the Cleveland Browns, to join the NFL ranks in 1950. Sensing a bonanza at the gate and a chance to validate their exalted position at the top of the pro football food chain, the NFL scheduled a showdown between the NFL-best Philadelphia Eagles and the AAFC-best Cleveland Browns to kick off the 1950 season.

The game was scheduled for Saturday, September 16, 1950—one day before the rest of the NFL teams played their openers. To tip the scales in the Eagles' favor, the game was played in Philadelphia.

The football world awaited the super-duper 1950 season opener. To allow as many fans as possible to witness the whuppin', the contest was played in Philadelphia's now-departed Municipal Stadium. Advance ticket sales were huge.

The Browns finished 5–0 in their five-game preseason exhibition schedule. None of the games, all played against NFL competition, were close. The scores were 38–7, 34–7, 35–14, 27–23, and 41–31. But the experts noted they were all meaningless exhibitions. None of the teams that fell to the Browns could match the talent of the Philadelphia Eagles.

To the dismay and disbelief of Philadelphia and the NFL the Browns blew the mighty Eagles off the field. In front of 71,237 stunned Eagles fans, the Browns rolled up 448 total yards and made mincemeat of the same Eagles defense that threw up goose eggs in the previous two NFL championship tilts.

The Eagles' dynasty died that night. The Eagles as contenders went slip-sliding away for the remainder of the fifties in almost eerie lock step with the Whiz Kids.

On October 7, precisely three weeks later, the Phils dropped their fourth World Series game in a row to the Yanks. Philly's brief bright 1950 glow was reduced to a flicker. Out, out brief candle.

Dalton Gang was headed after the game. I was too young, and honestly, I was too dull for those guys. I never knew where the Dalton Gang would be riding or hiding out every night.

"Tom Ferrick, a pitching coach the year before I got here [in 1960], came up with the Dalton Gang name. At least that's what I've been told. Del Ennis filled me in on the Dalton Gang. Del was a former Whiz Kid. He and I were teammates for half a season on the '59 Go-Go White Sox, as we were called. It always struck me funny that Del played on teams with wild-sounding names: the Whiz Kids and the Go-Go Sox. Yet Del was the most laid-back guy you could meet! Although Del and I were teammates on the '59 White Sox, neither of us played in that World Series. Del was released before the '59 All-Star Game and then called it a career. But he was a seasoned vet and taught me a lot in the short time we were teammates.

"That December when I was traded to the Phils, I called Del up because he still had lots of friends on the Phillies. He was born and raised in Philadelphia and played most of his career here. He gave me lots of good advice and one thing he told me was, 'John, you're a kid with a promising future [Callison was only 20 at the time]. Don't get hooked up with that Dalton Gang!'"

Good advice. The year Callison arrived in Philly was the year the Dalton Gang burst on to the national scene. For the most part in those days, stories that reflected poorly on sport heroes were hushed. But the Dalton Gang's shenanigans one Saturday night early in the 1960 season in Pittsburgh leaked out to the public. At that point, after only 37 games in a 154-game season, the Phils were already a hopeless 12½ games behind the front-runners.

Late on a Saturday night, Meyer and his teammate, Harry "the Horse" Anderson, were drinking at a watering hole near their hotel in the Iron City. A couple of sportswriters, Allen Lewis and Ray Kelly, along with Phillies broadcaster Byrum Saam sat nearby. Meyer was holding court on the topic of racehorses. As Meyer got louder and louder, Lewis, sensing trouble, tried to quiet him down. Meyer grew furious and started mouthing off to Lewis. Harry Anderson hustled Meyer back to the hotel. They put Meyer to bed. However, Turk Farrell, not content to let sleeping Daltons lie, suggested that it would be entertaining to dump a pitcher of ice water on Meyer. Farrell's motion was seconded by the rest of the Daltons, who agreed it would be hilarious. Denied a vote, Meyer expressed a minority dissent. He popped up cursing and fighting. Again Harry the Horse, along with pitcher John Buzhardt, managed to calm down Meyer and get him back to bed.

Shortly afterward, Meyer received a phone call. For reasons unknown, the call set him off again. Meyer stormed around the room, ripping down Venetian blinds, smashing radios, and trying to fight teammates. Somehow and somewhere during the course of his meltdown, Meyer hurt his back.

The next day, the story was out.

CALLISON: "I heard what happened. I wanted to stay as far away from trouble as possible. I remember sitting there, wishing the clubhouse was a mile long and I was a mile away from Mauch. Jack told Mauch his back hurt. Next thing we know, Meyer was headed out of the clubhouse. Later, we found out Mauch sent him back to Philly to get his back checked out. Meyer landed on the disabled list, and then he got walloped with a fine."

And Meyer *did* get walloped.

Medically, Meyer had suffered a herniated disk. Financially, he was smitten with a $1,200 fine by Phillies GM John Quinn. Meyer hit the roof at the size of the fine, telling the press, "I'm not made of money! I've got a wife and kids to support. I don't have that kind of money!"

At the time, according to contemporary reports, Meyer's was the biggest fine in terms of percent of salary that was ever levied on a ballplayer. Babe Ruth was once fined $5,000, as was Ted Williams. But Ruth was making $80,000 and Williams $125,000 when they were fined. Meyer's 1960 salary was about $14,000. His fine amounted to about 9 percent of his entire salary.

Meyer sang, as they called it in those days. He complained publicly, and the press ate it up. He demanded to be traded. He said he was getting a lawyer. He said he would quit baseball. He asked owner Bob Carpenter for his unconditional release.

Reporters swarmed manager Mauch, asking whether or not Meyer would be traded. "Meyer's a problem," Mauch shot back. "Do you think anybody wants to take a problem off my hands?"

Mauch had changed his tune. Striving to set a tone of fairness and glasnost when he first arrived in the Quaker City, when questioned about the Dalton Gang Gene Mauch said, "They're really not a problem as far as I'm concerned." Within three weeks, he ratcheted that answer up to, "Some of these guys are taking liberties."

Mauch knew some of the Gang's history. Only the Daltons knew the entire history, although they may not have been able to recall it all. In '59, Farrell was fined when he smashed a barroom mirror. As for Jim Owens, well, the Bear was a special case.

JOE LONNETT: "I was a teammate with these guys from '56 through '59. They were something! I knew the Bear pretty well. I was a scrub catcher behind starter Carl Sawatski. We also had Valmy Thomas and Jim Hegan, so my main job was to work with the young arms. That I could do. It was working with their young heads that I couldn't do! Jim Owens had major league stuff. But off the field, it was a different story. Our GM contracted with Jim to give him a $500 bonus if Jim behaved. Imagine that! And $500 was a good chunk of change in those days. Wanna know how far that deal went before falling through? Owens was in a barroom scuffle in Florida in *spring training*. He lost his bonus before we even started the season, and he was fined a $100, to boot! Then Owens had this big incident where he quit—for one day. He told the press he was the kind of pitcher who could stay up all night drinking and then go out and throw a shutout. He wasn't. Well, he didn't have a bad career, but he really could have been a good pitcher if he had stuck to the straight and narrow."

The Dalton Gang had no common link except a love of wild times. Meyer's family was fairly well off. Jack graduated from Philly's prestigious

Penn Charter School and Duke University. Farrell was a New Englander who had polio as a child and forever walked with a slight limp. Owens came from a broken home with a drinking, abusive father.

Over the years, the Dalton Gang enlisted some of the other young arms that flitted in and out of the swinging door that was the Phillies roster in those dark days.

Saul Rogovin, Seth Morehead, Warren Hacker, Tom "Money Bags" Qualters, and Al "Bull" Schroll, whose major league career included four teams in four years—all were reputed to have ridden with the Dalton Gang on occasion.

The Dalton Gang's reign of mischief lasted from 1956–61. By 1961, the new sheriff, manager Gene Mauch, had his fill of the Daltons. After the '61 season, both Farrell and Meyer were gone. After a 0–0, 9.00 ERA start in 1961 as a major leaguer, Jack Meyer belonged to the ages. Mauch dumped him in April. Farrell was dumped in May, sent to the Dodgers in a trade that brought Don Demeter to the Phils. At the end of the '61 season, the Houston Colt 45's drafted Turk as their fourth pick in the ($125,000) premium phase of the 1961 expansion draft.

Owens stayed in Mauch's doghouse through the '62 season. Then he was dealt to Cincy for Cookie Rojas, who became a popular, productive performer on the mid-sixties teams. Ironically, Owens was drafted by Houston in the Rule 5 draft. There the Bear reunited with ex–Dalton Ganger Turk Farrell. They remained teammates for four years.

Philadelphia always seems to welcome back prodigal sons. In 1967, Turk Farrell returned to Philadelphia where he closed out his career from 1967–69.

JOHN CALLISON: "There was a little bar near Connie Mack Stadium. The Dalton Gang used to sneak out or send somebody out to buy brews for them during the game. Mauch eventually found out and stopped it. All I know is Mauch wanted them to go. And he got rid of them quick after the big national Dalton Gang story. By '62, the Dalton Gang rode no more!"

YMCA

It pains me to say it, but I was a Yankees fan, but only briefly—for one year. You can't blame me. Any kid in the sixties would have been blown away after eating dinner with Mickey Mantle, Yogi Berra, Whitey Ford, Roger Maris, and Bobby Shantz.

Bobby Shantz was a friend of the family. When he was a kid, Shantzy used to pitch for Forest Hill Athletic Club in Northeast Philadelphia. My uncle, Rich Williamson, was his coach and mentor. Uncle Rich and Shantzy were bowling at the long-defunct Mayfair Bowling Alley when Uncle Rich suffered a heart attack and died in Shantzy's arms.

Uncle Rich's son, nicknamed Brud, was a couple decades older than me. He and Bobby were teammates at Forrest Hill and lifelong friends. In 1960 Brud took me to Yankee Stadium to meet his pal Bobby who was pitching for the Yanks at the time.

I watched the Baby Bird Baltimore Orioles beat the Bronx Bombers that day. The Baby Birds challenged the Yanks most of the season. Ultimately, Baltimore got chopped, and the Yanks won the pennant.

After the game, we met up for dinner with Shantz, his brother Wilmer (also a Yankee), Joe DeMaestri, and Tony Kubek, Bobby's roommate. Mickey Mantle and his Yankees posse of Whitey Ford and Roger Maris soon joined us, drinks in hand. Eventually, practically the entire Yankees team showed up at the bar-restaurant. They all came over and talked with me. At the time I didn't know that this was probably their first stop for a night on the town.

They gave me a baseball that every member of the 1960 Yankees signed. What a day!

When I started writing about baseball many years later, Bobby Shantz became a go-to guy for inside scoops. He was a wealth of information. When he was with the Yankees, Bobby Shantz also had an episode with a private investigator.

BOBBY SHANTZ: "I remember the story about Granny Hamner and the private investigator. I played with the A's in Philly when that stuff with Granny was going on. I had a good rapport with the Phillies. The A's and Phils played in the same park and used the same clubhouse. We also used to play a preseason series against each other right here in the city. It was a big rivalry.

"Using private investigators wasn't unusual in pro ball. The investigators just usually didn't get caught. Granny Hamner happened to catch this guy, and the whole thing blew up.

"When I was with the Yankees, Casey Stengel had a suspicion that guys were running wild after hours. He didn't care much until we hit a losing streak. That's when Casey hired some private eyes. He put one on me! I noticed a guy was tailing me! It seemed ridiculous because I was one of the cleanest-living guys on the Yankees—Bobby Richardson and I. Even the private eye wasn't taking his assignment seriously. I used to see him when I walked down to the hotel lobby. We started waving to each other. I'd go out every day to the YMCA, where I'd work out and practice diving, and he'd tail me."

Bobby wasn't exaggerating. He *was* Mr. Clean. He imbibed in moderation. But he was and is an early-to-bed, early-to-rise family man. As everyone in our family knows, he was a remarkable all-around athlete. To this day, he shoots golf in the 80s. In our family, his diving prowess is legendary. Bobby used to steal the show at Philly's Boulevard Pools when they had diving exhibitions. He was a terrific quarterback despite a 5'6", 150-lb. frame. I can personally attest to his ping-pong skills. He skunked me several times as a kid.

SHANTZ: "The whole private eye thing fizzled out. I never mentioned it to any of my teammates. And no one said anything to me, so I don't know who else was getting tailed. But the whole thing stopped when we started winning again."

Whither Wither

During the 1950s, the big question in Philadelphia was, "What happened?" After all, the Whiz Kids, in what should have been the breakout year for a potential dynasty, bested one of baseball's fabled teams, Brooklyn's Boys of Summer. The two teams parted paths after the 1950 showdown. Brooklyn ascended to baseball royalty. The Whiz Kids withered to the status of ephemeral anomalies, the second coming of the Miracle Braves—one-year wonders to whom history accords little respect.

Nonetheless, the team was built on Hall of Fame stock. Robin Roberts was the most dominant, consistent pitcher of the early fifties. Richie Ashburn was a two-time batting champ against stiff competition like Stan Musial, Willie Mays, and Hank Aaron. Del Ennis was a three-time All-Star; Willie Jones a two-time All-Star; Granny Hamner was a three-time All-Star who placed in the top 35 for MVP six times. Stan Lopata was an All-Star catcher. So was Smoky Burgess, who batted .368 in 1954 and was traded away the following season.

So why the disappointing finishes in the fifties? Whither the Whiz Kids?

RICH "WHITEY" ASHBURN, Hall of Fame center fielder and longtime broadcaster: "I won't say anything against the Carpenters [the Phillies' owners in Ashburn's playing days]. They lifted up the whole franchise. They saved it, in fact. If the Carpenters hadn't taken over the Phils, the A's would have been Philadelphia's team. Economics would have driven the Phillies somewhere else. That would have been the end of the Phillies brand name for sure. They wouldn't have been the Kansas City Phillies.

"The Carpenters handed out all that bonus-baby money. In the late forties, the bonuses were all paying dividends. Robbie [$25,000], Curt [$65,000], Willie Jones [$20,000], Granny Hamner [$9,500], and Stan Lopata [$25,000], and basically the entire nucleus of the Whiz Kids signed with Philly because of Carpenter bonus money. It was the first time the Phillies ever competed with the Yanks and some of the other richer teams."

To show the market value of the Phillies franchise back then, in 1943 the Carpenters bought the Phils for $200,000—a sum less than the $225,000 the Reds paid the Washington Senator's owner, Clark Griffith, for one guy! The guy happened to be Griffith's future son-in-law and future Hall of Famer Joe Cronin. Talk about your franchise players!

RICHIE ASHBURN: "The smartest thing the Carpenters did was to hire Herb Pennock as the GM. Herb believed the '40s-era Red Sox built their team the wrong way. They bought established stars, guys like Joe Cronin. Herb convinced the Carpenters to build the team bottom up—to sign promising kids and entice them with bonus checks. In those days, there were rules that major league teams couldn't tamper with kids in high school. So the Phillies had scouts all over the country who showed up at graduation ceremonies and opened their checkbooks up wide.

"The biggest setback the Phils ever took, in my opinion, was when Pennock died of a brain hemorrhage in January 1948. He was a real baseball man, and that's what the Carpenters needed. Pennock knew talent. The guys we signed on his watch turned into All-Stars. But once he was gone, we didn't sign talent. I won't say anything against Teddy Kazanski, but Teddy got $50,000 and never played up to major league par. Do you know the Phils had to choose between Al Kaline [a future Hall of Famer] and Kazanski? They picked Kazanski, and Teddy was really the only bonus baby after the initial batch who played any length of time in the fifties. Nobody else really came through."

When Herb Pennock died, Bob Carpenter took his place. In fact, Bob Carpenter took over the entire Phillies front office from 1948–53. He wasn't even 30 years of age. Carpenter had been a decent baseball player himself. He often worked out with the team. The players called him Bob. But he got too close to the field operations. He interfered. To a great extent, he usurped the role of the manager and took over the disciplining, thus undermining the manager's role.

RICHIE ASHBURN: "There was a big change from '50 to '51. I honestly believe we had too much success too soon. We were a bunch of

Catchless

SHANTZ: "I was supposed to be a reliever when I came to the Yankees, but Casey put me into the starting rotation because Whitey Ford was on the disabled list. I was 9–1 at the All-Star break and made the All-Star team. I had tremendous offensive support playing on a team with Mickey Mantle, Yogi Berra, Elston Howard, and the like.

"Back in those days, each ballpark was different. Each one had its own quirks, and each ballpark determined how a pitcher had to pitch, how a team would be built, and how a team would play the game itself.

"One day, we were playing the Red Sox in Fenway Park. Because of that short left-field fence and because I was a lefty, the Red Sox would load up their lineup against me with right-handed hitters. All those righties would try to pull everything I threw, and I'd try to keep everything low and away and get them to hit ground balls to the right side of the infield. Well, in this particular game, I got off to a rocky start. The Sox had Jimmy Piersall, Frank Malzone, and Jackie Jenson at the top of their lineup—all righties. Ted Williams was right behind them. Williams batted

young guys who, I think, started thinking this baseball thing was going to be easy. Our manager, Eddie Sawyer, was an easy-going guy. He gave us free rein, and a lot of guys took advantage.

"We had some incidents that put Sawyer on the outs with the players. Once in 1949, Sawyer clamped down when he thought certain guys were playing too hard off the field and dogging it on the field. After that, some guys never respected him. They never forgave him. They called him the Boy Scout. The name stuck. You know what they were mad about? He knew guys were out late beyond curfew and then sleeping late afterward. So he set a rule that players would have to get their $6 meal ticket in person from Frank Wiechec by 8:30 AM or they would forfeit it. Until then, they were just turning slips in for petty cash every day and left-handed, but it didn't matter who was pitching. Ted could hit any pitch from anybody. He's still the greatest batter I ever saw. Anyway, Piersall slapped my first pitch for a single. The next guy hit my first pitch for a double, and the third guy ripped my first pitch for another double. Out of the dugout comes Casey Stengel headed toward the mound.

"Casey had a habit of intercepting the catcher on his way to the mound. Casey wanted a little insight from the catcher before he 'discussed' matters with the pitcher. Besides, our catcher, Yogi Berra, was the best field general I ever saw in baseball. Casey grabs Yogi about 15' away from the mound. I've got my back to them, facing away because I didn't want to get yanked out of this thing so early. I always wondered about that expression, 'yanked.' It probably didn't come from the way the Yankees yanked pitchers out of games faster than anybody else, but it should have!

"Anyway, this was not the start of the game that either Casey or I envisioned. So I hear Casey ask Yogi, 'What's goin' on? Doesn't Shantzy have anything today?' Yogi answers, 'How would I know? I haven't caught one yet!'"

---

pocketing the money. But all he was really doing was, in a roundabout way, trying to snuff out the late-night carousing.

"In 1951, some of our players kind of acted like we had won the World Series in 1950. That didn't sit well with Eddie or the Carpenters. At spring training, some guys were going AWOL to fish and faking being sick so they could hang by the pool all day. Management, particularly Sawyer, didn't know how to deal with it. Then things got worse. We brought in Steve O'Neill to manage. O'Neill was considered too easy on ballplayers everywhere he managed. Our team went in the opposite direction of what we needed."

In 1952, the 28–35 Phils who had faltered under Sawyer finished strong (59–32) under O'Neill. O'Neill continued at the helm in '53 when the Phillies scrambled up to third place, their highest finish in the fifties other than the pennant year.

RICHIE ASHBURN: "I won't say the front office panicked in '54. But there's no question there was a lot of concern that the Whiz Kids were not realizing their potential. To make matters worse, none of the bonus babies were panning out, either."

By the time the Whiz Kids won the 1950 pennant, the Phillies had already paid out a whopping, MLB-leading $850,000 in bonuses. Aside from the initial batch that became the Whiz Kids, the rest of the bonus-baby crop withered on the vine.

RICHIE ASHBURN: "In '54, the organization took another hit. Bob Carpenter decided to relinquish the GM job to Roy Hamey. On the surface, it seemed like a good step. Hamey had a history of success in his baseball front-office operations. In the twenties, he was a business manager in the minors. Then he spent years in the Yankee system. He was a minor league president [American Association]. And when the Phils hired him, he had been working for George Weiss, the Yankee GM who built those great Yankee teams.

"All that experience didn't translate into success in Philadelphia. As soon as he got here, he made it his mission to clamp down on some of our wild guys. Word gets around fast in MLB. Everybody knew that some of the Whiz Kids liked the good life. So Hamey set out to get the team in line. He hired a private investigator to tail Granny Hamner. Granny was driving home one night from a night game. He spotted a car on his tail. When he got home, he looked out and saw the car circle the street and then park across from his house. Granny called the cops. The cops came and found a guy with his wife and a loaded .38 next to them sitting in the car. There was another gun in the back seat. The guy made up this phony story that he was trailing somebody else and got the cars mixed up.

"Carpenter headed down to the station to post bail on the private eye, and word got out. Hamner was furious. So were many others. Then the Phils brought in Terry Moore as manager. He clamped down even more on the players. Moore was a former member of St. Louis' Gas House

Gang. The Phils botched his hiring, too. They let it get out that he was an interim manager. Huge mistake! Some players treated Terry like a substitute teacher."

The front office considered the Phils underachievers. When Hamner was asked if he agreed with that assessment, Hamner, who was still steamed about the private eye incident, told the press, "We're in fourth place because the first three clubs have better players."

Terry Moore announced he was going to fine Hamner for dissension, which angered Hamner even more. Hamey got wind that some of the players were bragging that the players got Sawyer and O'Neill fired, and Moore was in their cross-hairs.

However, to try to restore some order, the players met and drafted a statement that everyone but Hamner signed: "The statements made in the press recently about our ball club were strictly the personal opinion of one player and do not represent the feelings of the rest of our squad. We have too much respect for our manager, Terry Moore, to let this go unanswered. We hope the future results on the field will bear out our feelings."

The whole mess contributed to the ultimate unraveling of the Whiz Kids.

RICHIE ASHBURN: "They were tumultuous times. Everything seemed to combine to destroy the spirit and camaraderie we had in 1950. We never recovered, and the Whiz Kids were never serious contenders again."

Granny

In 1993, Granville Wilbur "Granny" Hamner, who joined the major leagues at age 17 and played shortstop for the Philadelphia Phillies during the 1940s and '50s, was found dead in his Philadelphia hotel room. He was 66. Hamner, who was living in Paulsboro, New Jersey, at the time, suffered a heart attack. He was attending a sports memorabilia and card show in Philadelphia.

Hamner, a 17-year veteran, was an All-Star from 1952–54. He was the Phils' starting shortstop in 1952 and starting second baseman in

Granny Hamner was honored by Richmond fans and talks to (l to r) Otis Belcher, Joe McGinnis, and Richmond mayor T. Nelson Parker at the Granny Day celebration on September 18, 1950, in Shibe Park, Philadelphia. *(AP Photo)*

1954, becoming the first player in All-Star history to start at two different positions. He was traded to Cleveland in 1959 and retired in 1962. His 21-year-old brother, Wesley Garvin Hamner, played 32 games for the 1945 Phillies team.

PUTSY CABALLERO: "Can you imagine a major league game where there's a 16-year-old at third base and a 17-year-old at shortstop? Well, it happened. That's how Granny Hamner and I broke in. Let me tell you, son, that baseball diamond was a really strange place during the war years! You could never be sure what you were going to see out there."

Putsy was the 16 year-old at third in that story. Granny Hamner was the 17-year-old shortstop. On September 14, 1944, the two teens entered a 2-hour, 2-minute game at the Polo Grounds approximately 1 hour, 45 minutes into the game. The contest drew all of 1,668 spectators. Most of them had departed the scene—a lopsided 12–1 affair in the Giants' favor—by the time the Philly teens were inserted in the seventh inning.

PUTSY: "Our debuts weren't very grand. We both made weak outs in our only plate appearances. Freddie Fitzsimmons was our manager. Freddie was a big-name pitcher the whole time I was growing up. It was intimidating enough to be 16 in the clubhouse with a big name like Fitzsimmons. And the Giants had some really intimidating names too, like the three guys in the middle of their lineup: Mel Ott, Ducky Medwick, and Ernie Lombardi. All three wound up in the Hall of Fame. Ott was the player-manager. Granny and I broke in against a 20-game winner out on the hill—a big pitcher named Bill Voiselle. Voiselle was great that year. But he kind of faded once all the big-name guys came back from the war.

"As for me and Granny, we were two southern boys coming up and playing in the big city. Being in New York City was a little intimidating for a couple of teenagers like us. Neither of us had ever seen anything like New York."

After their debut, Granny Hamner became the starting shortstop. He started all 20 of the games that remained that season. The Phils won six in a row. Then they came back down to earth. They lost nine straight. Such ups and downs marked the rhythm of Granny Hamner's career.

RICHIE ASHBURN: "Granny Hamner was a full-blown, colorful character! We roomed together in the mid-1950s. Now I could tell you some Granny Hamner stories. But there's a lot more Granny Hamner stories I couldn't tell you."

On August 8, 1987, Granny Hamner was inducted into the Philadelphia Sports Hall of Fame along with Eddie Collins of the

Philadelphia A's. The ceremony was part of the Equitable Old Timers Night at the Vet. The festivities included an exhibition game with the stars of the Phils from the late 1950s, including Richie Ashburn, Robin Roberts, Del Ennis, Pancho Herrera, Granny, and others against a late-fifties-era All-Star team (or so it was billed, but late-fifties was more like an approximation) that included Hall of Famers Willie Mays, Bob Gibson, Ernie Banks, Bob Feller, Luke Appling, Bobby Doerr, and Enos Slaughter. I had a chance to catch up with Granny that night and to gingerly ask him about his statement to the press that the Phils' talent didn't measure up to the NL elites.

GRANNY HAMNER: "Yeah, I said it. I meant it. I didn't think it would cause such a stink. We just weren't matching the young talent the other teams were bringing in Willie Mays, Eddie Mathews, Hank Aaron, Ernie Banks, Minnie Minoso, Larry Doby, Jackie Jensen, Mickey Mantle, and the like. As for 1950, hell, I still can't believe we won that year, either! I think back to that season a lot. It was the highlight of my 17 years as a player, and I'll tell you, I really don't know how we won it. We were maybe the fourth-best team in the league that year.

"But we didn't know any better. We were young, and we battled. We were the Phightin' Phils. We didn't have stars, except for Robbie. We didn't have great ballplayers like Duke Snider, Roy Campanella, and Jackie Robinson. But we had a solid team and camaraderie. Things fell in place until the end of the season when everything almost came apart. Luckily Sisler's home run put us over the top. I thank God he hit that one! Otherwise, this town would be crucifying the '50 Phils instead of the '64 team."

Hamner had a career many veterans would gladly trade for. He set Phils records (that have since been broken) for most homers by a shortstop (17 in 1952) and second baseman (21 in 1953.) Granny was also the first player ever voted an All-Star starter by the fans at two different positions.

HAMNER: "Pete Rose was voted in at just about every position after I was out of baseball. But I was the first guy ever picked at both second and short. And I have a confession to make—I was a lousy second baseman! But in '53, I got off to my best year ever with the stick. I was hitting well around All-Star time. My bat got me into the lineup. It sure as hell wasn't my glove! I had started the All-Star Game as a shortstop in '52. I finished second in voting for second baseman. Red Schoendienst started. It's no shame getting beat out by a Hall of Famer. But then in '54, I started at second base and Schoendienst was *my* backup."

Those three years, 1952, '53, and '54, were Hamner's zenith. Granny batted .275, .276, and .299 with 17, 21, and 13 homers and 87, 92, and 89 RBIs—excellent production for a middle infielder in that era.

In 1954, Hamner—at only 27 years of age—was already a 10-year MLB vet. He was conceivably en route to a Hall of Fame career. But over the next three years, his average tanked to .257, .224, and .227. Injuries derailed his career. A damaged left shoulder in 1956 ruined his swing, and in May 1958 he tore up a knee, which sounded the death knell for his days as a star.

ROBIN ROBERTS: "Granny was a tough player, but injuries did him in. He hurt his leg, and once that happened, he had no mobility. But in his early years he was special. He had a phenomenal arm at short, and he made the DP relay as well as I've ever seen it done. He was a natural at short and a decent second baseman. Most of all, I can't think of anybody I'd rather have at the plate with a game on the line. He could be 0-for-3 and look overmatched all day long. But put a man in scoring position in the eighth inning, and he'd hit a rope someplace."

chapter 3

Dodgers

Name Changers

"Snakes! Why does it always have to be snakes?"

Snakes were Indiana Jones' nemesis, his archenemy, the villain who always stood between Indy and the prize. That's what the Dodgers are to the Phils. They're always in the way. To thin-skinned Dodgers fans reading this, I'm in no way comparing Dodgers to snakes. One is a misunderstood, maligned yet noble creature that fills an essential ecological niche by helping to regulate rodent populations. The other plays NL baseball.

As fate would have it, the Dodgers were conceived in 1883, the same year the Phillies entered the National League. But they weren't called the Dodgers at the time. They were called the Brooklyn Graze in homage to Don Drysdale's pitching style—I kid. They were the Brooklyn Grays, and they won the Inter-State Association of Professional Baseball Clubs title their very first year. Suffice it to say, the 17–81 eighth-place Phillies' NL debut was less successful.

The Grays jumped to the American Association in 1884. In 1888, they changed their name to the Brooklyn Bridegrooms because several team members got married about the same time.

The Bridegrooms joined the National League in 1890 and promptly won the NL pennant, becoming the first pro team to win consecutive championships in two different leagues.

After a few seasons as the Grooms and a few others as the Bridegrooms, they became the Brooklyn Superbas, winning NL pennants in 1899 and 1900. It wasn't until 1911 that they became the Dodgers for the first time. Brooklynites at the turn of the twentieth century were derided by their uptown Manhattan neighbors as "trolley dodgers," hence the Dodgers name.

The Dodgers promptly tanked in the standings. Our Phils topped them practically every year until finally, in 1915, the Phils claimed the franchise's first pennant. The Dodgers, by the way, had ditched the Dodgers name in 1914 in favor of the Robins, selected to honor their manager Wilbert Robinson. For the better part of the next three decades, Brooklyn and Philadelphia tracked each other in the standings—the bottom part of the standings.

The first time Brooklyn played snake to the Phillies' Indiana Jones was the year after the Phils' 1915 pennant. The Phils were favored to repeat, but Brooklyn edged them out and won the NL flag by 2½ games.

In 1917, it was the Phils who played bridesmaids—not to the former Bridegrooms of Brooklyn, but to John McGraw's New York Giants. Brooklyn tumbled to seventh. The 1918 Phillies, *sans* Grover Cleveland Alexander and the 30 wins he gave them for three straight seasons, plummeted to sixth. The following year, they hit the cellar and stuck or stunk, remaining in either last or next-to-last place every year until 1929.

The Robins didn't fare much better. Inexplicably, they sneaked into a pennant in 1920. However, Brooklyn's twenties, like the Phillies', were roar-less. The Robins went south every summer, nesting in sixth every year but two in the twenties. Their goofy personnel and erratic play earned them the nickname the "Daffiness Boys."

Once again, throughout the thirties, the Phils and Brooklyn vied for NL's worst franchise. They remained practically tethered at the bottom of the standings. Six times one finished directly behind the other, always in the second division.

Brooklyn's major achievement in the thirties came in 1932, the year after Wilbert Robinson retired. They finally became the Dodgers for good—well, more like forever than for good. Presumably, they will remain the Dodgers unless one of the current owners campaigns for a name-change to the Magic. Believe it or not, Brooklyn once tinkered with becoming the Canaries in honor of new manager Max Carey, whose birth name was Canarius.

The forties were a new decade for both the Dodgers and the Phils. In 1940, Brooklyn finished second. The following year, Brooklyn won the pennant. The Phils gifted the Dodgers with Dolph Camilli, who led the NL in home runs and RBIs and won the MVP Award. Meanwhile back in Philadelphia, the Phils were 43–111 and finished the season 57 games back.

In 1940, the big change agents arrived—men whose programs would set the Phils and Dodgers on a collision course to a showdown. Branch Rickey arrived in Brooklyn in 1942, replacing Larry MacPhail as Dodgers president and GM. A few years later, Rickey engineered baseball's biggest, boldest innovation ever when he signed Jackie Robinson to a contract and broke baseball's color barrier. To underscore how bold and revolutionary Rickey's undertaking was in its time, consider this— Rickey integrated baseball before the U.S. integrated its armed forces.

The times, they were a-changin' for the Phils, too. In 1943, Robert Ruliph Morgan Carpenter, a scion of the DuPont family, bought the perennially cash-strapped Phillies. For the first time, a Phillies owner was spending money on the team.

Carpenter's spending started paying dividends as the late forties unfolded. Suddenly, the only two NL franchises that had never won a World Championship were picking up steam. The Dodgers, turbo-charged from the African Americans on their roster, were the first to taste success when they won the pennant in 1947 and 1949. But the Phils' young bonus babies blossomed the following year, and Brooklyn and Philadelphia were headed for an exciting showdown on the last day of the 1950 season. In the ensuing years, many more such contests were in store for the two franchises. And although the Phils jousted for the NL pennant with Houston in 1980, the Reds in 1976 and 2010, and the Braves in 1993, their final step to every other pennant they won—1950, 1977, 1978, 2008, and 2009—required getting by the Dodgers.

Dodgers! Dodgers! Why does it always have to be Dodgers?

Kids-Boys

MAJE McDONNELL, Whiz Kids coach: "The day we won the pennant in 1950 was the greatest day of my life."

Maje used to gush whenever he talked about the glory days of Ashburn, Roberts, Ennis, and Simmons. Maje was a 30-year-old coach for the 1950 Whiz Kids.

MAJE: "For most of the '50 season, everything went our way. The Carpenters, the new owners, wanted to build a strong minor league system that constantly replenished the aging talent on the parent club. By 1950, the Phillies' lineup was fully stocked with 'bonus babies.'" They then went through the Phils' minor league system and came up to the Phillies.

"Ennis and Simmons were locals. Ennis was born and raised in Philly. Simmons hailed from around Bethlehem. By being young and home-grown, the '50 Phils were the darlings of Philadelphia. I think the only team fans might have loved more was the 1993 Phillies. The 1980 and 2008 Phillies won the World Series, but I don't think they connected with fans the same way. Both the Whiz Kids and the Beards, Bellies and Biceps crew had some real characters. Both teams were entertaining on and off the field!"

For the first and only time since their 1915 pennant-winning season, the Phils led the National League in attendance, wooing Philadelphia Athletics' fans to desert the A's for the first time. The A's reeled from the lost gate receipts. The lost revenue sounded their death knell. Philadelphia simply wasn't a town big enough for the two of them.

MAJE: "The Whiz Kids came along in the period right after the Big War. Before the war, almost every big city was in the northeast. But the country grew fast after the war. Urban centers sprang up in other parts of the country. Connie Mack, the manager and owner of the A's, started looking for more profitable cities."

The Whiz Kids took over first place toward the end of July and held fast. Brooklyn pursued resolutely, but by September 17 the Phils had stretched out their lead over the Dodgers to a comfortable 7½ games with

Del Ennis powers the ball to deep right field in the fifth inning of a game against the Reds on August 23, 1950, in Cincinnati. Cincinnati catcher John Pramesa looks on. *(AP Photo)*

only 13 games to play. But all was not as peachy as it seemed. Trouble was festering in Philly. Curt Simmons was called up to active military duty in September. Filling his roster spot was the eminently forgettable Jocko Thompson who appeared in only two games and pitched only four innings. Hurler Bob Miller was hurt. Miller had started the '50 campaign at a blistering 8–0 pace. Then in a freak accident, he injured his arm carrying a suitcase at Philadelphia's 30th Street Station. He limped through the rest of the season at a 3–6 clip. Another starter, Bubba Church, was winged by a Ted Kluszewski line drive and was ineffective thereafter.

MAJE: "The Bob Miller accident was so weird. I was walking with Bob on the steps at the train station. They were wet, and he slipped. He couldn't even get up. He hurt his back bad. We finally got him comfortable, but the poor guy never recovered. He had a promising future, but he was never the same pitcher again.

"When we hit the final two weeks of the season, everything landed on Robin Roberts' shoulders. Everybody in Philadelphia remembers Short and Bunning handling the load in 1964. That was nothing compared to how often Sawyer pitched Robbie. Roberts would take that ball anytime the manager handed it to him. He started three games in the last five days of the regular season. Can you imagine that nowadays! By the last game of the season, our 7½ game lead had dwindled down to a single game. And—what could be more dramatic?—our final game of the season was against the team that was one game behind us, the Dodgers!

"Robbie squared off again against Don Newcombe. Here's more drama—they were both going for their 20th win that day! That Roberts-Newcombe rivalry is still the best I ever saw in baseball. All through the 1950s those two battled each other. I never saw guys with more mutual respect and pride."

Before Newk called it a career, he became the first and only player (until Justin Verlander accomplished the same trifecta) ever to win Rookie of the Year, MVP, and the Cy Young Award. Newcombe, in fact, was the first-ever Cy Young Award recipient. And although Roberts and the Whiz Kids thwarted his 1950 quest for 20 wins, in 1951 Newk became the first African American ever to win 20 games in a season. In 1952, he became the first African American to start a World Series game, and in 1956, he was the first pitcher to win the MVP and Cy Young Award in the same season.

MAJE McDONNELL: "Don't forget Newk was one of the finest hitting pitchers ever. He swung a mean bat, although there used to be a bunch of good-hitting pitchers like Warren Spahn, Bob Lemon, and Early Wynn. For the most part, that aspect of the game has disappeared. What a shame, although I think the best-hitting pitcher I've seen is this guy Carlos Zambrano who's playing now. That man can hit a ball a long way.

"The final game for the pennant in 1950 was a typical Roberts-Newcombe duel. It was a hot day. That helped Robbie. He was always tougher in hot weather, and this day was really unseasonably hot [the thermometer hit 88.4 degrees at 3:45 PM, which broke a record set in 1881].

"We were leading 1–0 in the sixth. Pee Wee Reese, the Dodgers' [Veteran's Committee] future Hall of Fame shortstop, hit a cheap homer. The ball lodged in a screen along the right-field wall. Robbie fooled Pee Wee on the pitch, but in that little bandbox, Pee Wee got enough of it to *almost* put it out. Point is, He *didn't* hit it out. But the umps ruled he did.

"Robbie and Newk were both dealing. It was 1–1 in the ninth. We didn't score in our half. When the Dodgers came to bat, I thought Ebbets Field was going to explode. Cal Abrams had a terrific at-bat and worked Robbie for a walk. Our whole bench was up and screaming at the call. It didn't help. Never does, right? Abrams wound up on first as the potential winning run. Up comes Pee Wee again—one of the best bunters *ever* to play this game. He missed two bunt tries then lined a single to center, and things were starting to look bad.

"Suddenly there were two on, no one out, and the Duke of Brooklyn at the plate. Let me tell you, Duke Snider, just like Richie Ashburn, didn't get enough credit. He was just as good as the other two center fielders in the 'Willie, Mickey, and the Duke' song. Anyway, he lined the first pitch to Richie Ashburn in center. Richie was charging the ball at 100 mph at the crack of the bat. Ashburn got the best jump on a baseball I ever saw. He gloved it and threw a perfect strike to the plate. Any other day, Abrams scores on that play. But Richie's throw was perfect. Abrams was out.

"There's still no breathing room. Jackie Robinson was next up, followed by Carl Furillo, who grew up in Reading. Robbie walked Robinson. But Furillo popped up to Eddie Waitkus at first, and Gil Hodges flew out to right to end the inning.

"I knew right then and there we were going to win. Sure enough, the top of the 10th was pure magic! Dick Sisler hit a three-run homer. I'm prejudiced, but that was the most magic moment in Phillies history, probably because I thought so highly of Dick Sisler. What a gentleman! Dick was the son of George Sisler, a great Hall of Famer. No matter what Dick did, he could never measure up to what his dad accomplished. George Sisler was special. He had 257 hits in 1920—a record that stood until Ichiro broke it in 2004. But did you know he also studied engineering at Michigan?

"Anyway, I have to tell you a funny story about Dick. He was very shy, and he stuttered. I drove up to Brooklyn with him for that final Dodgers series. We stopped for gas. As it turned out, the gas station attendant stuttered. The attendant says to Dick, 'H-h-h-h-ello, c-c-c-c-an I f-f-f-ill 'er up?' When Dick stuttered back, 'Sh-sh-sh-ure! F-f-f-ill 'er up!' the guy shook his head and walked away muttering, 'S-s-s-mart-ass!'"

"Dick wasn't our finest outfielder. He didn't take after his dad as a gloveman. Jackie Mayo replaced him in right in the bottom of the 10th. It didn't matter. Robbie mowed the Dodgers down one-two-three."

The victory gave the season a pleasing symmetry. The Whiz Kids won the season opener 9–1, Roberts beating Newcombe. The finale ended 4–1 with Roberts over Newcombe. After five consecutive failures to nail down his 20th win, Roberts succeeded and became the Phils' first 20-game winner since 1917 when Grover Cleveland Alexander won 30.

The future for the Phils looked so bright they had to wear shades. And it was the Phils who landed the first blow in the Dodgers wars.

Then Bowa Said to Schmidt

The Phightins fizzled in 1976. They were the first Phillies team to win 101 regular-season games, but Cincinnati's Big Red Machine burst that bubble and swept them in the NLCS.

In 1977, the Phils won 101 regular-season games again. This time their NLCS opponent was the Los Angeles Dodgers. The two split the regular season series 6–6 with the Phils scoring 52 runs and the Dodgers scoring 50. The Phils' prospects seemed brighter than the previous year. They now had playoff experience, plus the Dodgers didn't have the flash and star power of the Big Red Machine. Half the members of Cincinnati's starting eight had won at least one MVP Award—that's a daunting foe.

The Dodgers had made frequent postseason appearances since the Whiz Kids did them in. Five times in the fifties (four times as the Brooklyn Dodgers, once as L.A.), three times in the sixties, and once in the seventies, the Dodgers won pennants. In that span, the Phils won none—nada. Since 1950, the Phillies' sole appearance in the postseason was against the Cincinnati Reds in 1976. The Phils hadn't won a post-season game since the 1915 World Series, when they won only one. The Yankees swept them in four in the 1950 World Series, and the Reds swept them in three in the 1976 NLCS.

JERRY MARTIN, Phillies 1970s supersub outfielder: "I was blessed to get on the field in the Phillies' three '70s playoff series in '76, '77, and '78, even though things didn't go our way. When the Phils finally won the Series in '80, I was on the Cubs. I may not have been with the Phils, but I felt like I was! I was pulling for them all the way. I loved those guys.

"1976 was the first postseason experience for most of the Phils except for Lefty Carlton and Jim Lonborg. The Big Red Machine we faced that series were the defending world champs, and they were fearsome. We felt more confident in the '77 postseason.

"We took the '77 Series opener in L.A. behind Lefty. Our big guns fired right away. Bull homered in the first inning. We cruised until Cey hit a grand slam in the seventh to tie the score at five. In the ninth Schmitty singled, put us ahead, and the Tugger shut them down."

The Phils didn't know at the time that Schmidt's RBI would be his only RBI in the series.

In the next game, eventual NLCS MVP and lifelong Phils nemesis Dusty Baker socked another grand slammer to bury the Phils, setting the stage for one of Philadelphia's darkest days in any sport: Black Friday, October 7, 1977.

JERRY MARTN: "I'll never forget that day.

"We were winning in the ninth—no one on, two out, Gene Garber pitching. The Vet crowd was the loudest I ever heard, and that's saying something. Vic Davalillo pinch-hit for Steve Yeager and dragged a bunt toward second, which he beat out. After the game, Davalillo said he noticed that Ted Sizemore, our second baseman, was playing him very deep, and he took advantage of it.

"Manny Mota pinch-hit for Lance Rautzhan and drove one deep to left. Can you believe he did it on an 0–2 pitch? Greg Luzinski was in left. Bull reached for the ball, but it caromed off his glove. Then his throw to second skipped past Sizemore, and Davalillo advanced to third.

"Philadelphians have been arguing about that play ever since, blaming the manager [Danny Ozark] for not substituting me for Bull, who wasn't the best defensive player around. I might have caught Mota's fly. But who's to say? That's baseball. You never really know."

Despite Bull's play or misplay, the Phils retained a two-run advantage. They were still one lone out away from a win. Then Davey Lopes hit a blistering liner to third. It took a wicked hop and bounced off Schmidt's knee. An alert Larry Bowa at short grabbed the carom. He fired to first, and it arrived just in time to nip the fleet Lopes. However, umpire Bruce Froemming didn't see it that way. He ruled Lopes safe, which ignited a long, impassioned argument.

TUG McGRAW: "The most amazing thing I heard during that argument came from Schmidt. Everyone was screaming and hollering! Froemming was standing there scowling! Bowa was ballistic. 'He was [expletive] out!' Schmitty, the ultimate Mr. Cool, realized no amount of screaming was going to change Froemming's ruling, so Schmidt calmly

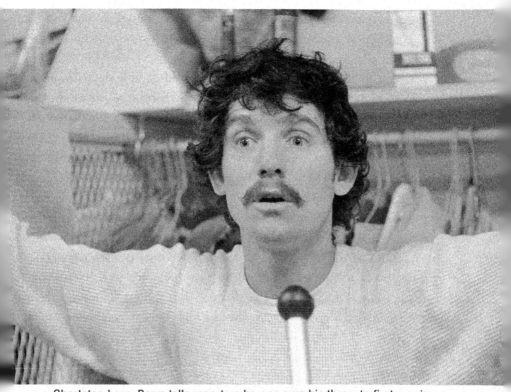

Shortstop Larry Bowa tells reporters he was sure his throw to first was in time to get the Dodgers' Davey Lopes out in ninth inning of the NL playoff game on Friday, October 7, 1977, in Philadelphia. Lopes was called safe, and the Dodgers were able to win the game 6–5. *(AP Photo)*

said to Bowa, 'He was safe.' Bowa looked at Schmidt like he was nuts and screamed, 'What the [expletive] are you talking about? Safe?' Schmitty, still calm, answered, 'Check the box score tomorrow. He was safe.' Then Bowa said to Schmidt—well, I won't tell you what he said. But it isn't something you'd hear at Sunday school.

"The nightmare inning got worse, almost surreal. I was watching from the pen and couldn't believe it was really happening.

"Now the game was tied 5–5. Garber always had a nice pickoff move. He tried it and fooled Lopes. Garber had him dead to rights, but he made an error and Lopes moved into scoring position. Russell followed with a single. Lopes scored, the Dodgers won 6–5, and instead of being up 2–1, we were one game away from elimination."

Actually the Phils had another shot at redemption in the bottom half of the frame. The 2-3-4 hitters batted in the bottom of the ninth. But Dodger Mike Garman induced a Bowa popup and a Schmidt fly out. They were down to the last out when Luzinski was hit by a pitch. Jerry Martin pinch-ran for him, which underscored Ozark's failure to insert Martin as a defensive replacement a half-inning earlier. Richie Hebner grounded out to first to end the game.

The Dodgers needed one more victory to take the flag. They got it the next night at the Vet in a driving rainstorm.

JERRY MARTIN: "In the second inning, Dusty Baker muscled one through a driving rain. I couldn't believe any ball could leave the park on a soggy ugly night like that. But that one did. Tommy John was tough that night. And for us it was just another wait-'til-next-year ending."

Wheeze

The 1983 Phils launched the franchise's second century of NL competition. A patched-up mosaic of aging Big Red Machiners teamed with a tiny contingent from the Phils' seventies juggernauts. The '83 Phils were dubbed the Wheeze Kids. The geezers were mediocre most of the year. Inexplicably, they got hot in September and, to the surprise of everyone, landed in the NLCS.

To be sure, the '83 Phils were loaded with big names like Schmidt, Rose, Morgan, Perez, and Carlton. Almost all of them ended up in the Hall of Fame. Never in franchise history had the Phillies boasted a roster with so many future Hall of Famers. Yes, the 33-year-old Mike Schmidt was still in his peak years, but the rest of the above quartet was a Phillies version of *The Expendables*—aged superstars who tapped experience rather than their dissipated skill to win. At 38 years of age, Carlton was the youngster of the quartet. Morgan was 39, Perez 41, and Rose 42.

The low level of performance on the playing field manifested itself in the All-Star roster. After years of placing three, four, or five Phillies on the All-Star squad, Mike Schmidt was the sole Phillies honoree. No one else came close to an All-Star berth. Despite all that, the Phils somehow limped into September at 67–64, just a game behind the leader. Then a Ruthian 22–7 September surge whizzed or wheezed them into a division championship, which set up another showdown— their third straight—against their perennial nemesis, the Dodgers. The Phils' prospects in this one weren't promising. The Phightins were 1–11 against the Dodgers. To make matters worse, the series was starting in L.A.

GARY "SARGE" MATTHEWS, Phils outfielder in the 1980s and current announcer: "That's why you play these games! They're not played on paper. It didn't matter what happened during the regular season. This was postseason. We had a clubhouse full of veterans. We knew what we had to do to win."

Matthews, or "Sarge," is well known to TV viewers of Phillies' games. Sarge provides color commentary, which is often entertaining merely because of Sarge's serendipitous accentuations and unusually syncopated rhythms.

SARGE: "The Dodgers may have won the season series, but we weren't afraid of them. Not one player on our team had any doubt we could beat them."

In Game 1, Mike Schmidt continued his mastery of Jerry Reuss when he tagged Reuss for a first-inning round-tripper. Schmidt roughed up Reuss for 10 homers in his illustrious career. Bob Forsch was the only pitcher he hit more against (11). Schmidt's home run was all Steve Carlton needed for a 1–0 victory.

SARGE: "Carlton was an all-time great and true professional. Lefty knew we needed to start this thing off with a win. We wanted to make a statement after we lost all those regular-season games to L.A. Another big motivator—even though I wasn't there myself—was that a lot of our guys were still fired up about losing twice to L.A. in the seventies.

Subpar

The 1978 Phils slipped. They fell far short of their two previous 101-win seasons. Big gun Mike Schmidt was subpar. After four straight 35+ HR seasons, Michael Jack's output tumbled to 21. His 78 RBIs were a career low, excluding his rookie season. The Bull, Greg Luzinski, socked 35 homers and drove in 101 runs, but his average dipped to .256 after three consecutive .300 seasons. Steve Carlton had a subpar—for him—16–13 record. Larry Christenson dropped off from 19–6 the previous season to 13–14. Despite their rash of subpar seasons, the Phils played the Dodgers almost even-up (5–7) in the regular season.

The '78 Phils had one advantage in the NLCS over the previous year—this series opened in Philly's jam-packed Veterans Stadium. Philly fans were thirsting for revenge, particularly since Burt Hooton got the Dodgers' starting nod for Game 1. Phillies fans had rattled Hooton in the 1977 NLCS. The Phils struck in the bottom of the second when Mike Schmidt, batting in the sixth hole, brought home Luzinski, who had tripled to open the frame, on a sacrifice fly. However, the Dodgers answered right away with a Garvey three-run home run off Larry Christenson that highlighted a four-run frame. The Dodgers added two more on a Lopes homer in the next inning. That was all the Dodgers needed en route to a 9–5 win.

In Game 2, Tommy John topped Dick Ruthven 4–0 on the strength of a Lopes' single, triple, and home run. Lopes collected one less hit than the entire Phillies' contingent could manage.

"Carlton came up with one of his dominant games in the opener. Schmitty hit that first-inning homer, and that was all Carlton needed."

Cy Young Award–winner John Denny took the mound in Game 2. Bowa's boot gave the Dodgers a one-run first-inning advantage, which Matthews nullified with one swing to open the second.

SARGE: "Yeah, for me, that was another statement. We wanted to show we were going to battle them every step of the way. The slate was clean now. The regular season didn't mean a thing."

When the series recommenced in L.A., Lefty kept the Phillies' hopes alive.

JERRY MARTIN: "Hey, don't forget I had a ninth-inning dinger in Game 1! I pinch-hit for McGraw and went yard on [Bob] Welch. Too little, too late—story of my life! In Game 3, Carlton did it all! Lefty socked a three-run home run off Sutton in the second. Then later, he drove in a couple more. I was the next batter and doubled Lefty in. We won 9–4, but that was our last hurrah."

In the Phils' second all-time postseason overtime loss, Philadelphia lost a long-ball slugfest. Homers by the Phils' Luzinski and Bake McBride and the Dodgers' Cey and Garvey resulted in a 3–3 deadlock in regulation. In the top of the tenth, after the heart of the Phillies' order failed, the Dodgers' Bill Russell hit a clutch single to ice the game and pennant for the Dodgers.

TUG McGRAW: "I'm happy the Phillies fans forgive and forget, because I hardly ever heard about that 1978 game after 1980. That image of the final strikeout of the World Series, with me jumping up and down, seemed to wipe out all previous memory! But, I'll be honest, that tenth inning I pitched in the '78 NLCS, well, I think that was probably my worst memory in Philly, personally. The city was so crazed when we won in 1980, everybody forgot that bummer. Still, I'm the one that lost that game for us. I was horrible. I didn't have a thing that day."

Fernando Valenzuela, however, didn't read the memo. He turned in a superb performance, outdueling Denny in a 4–1 Dodgers win that knotted the series at 1–1.

SARGE: "That next game was one of my personal best. We played on a Friday night. Bob Welch pitched for the Dodgers. Welch was the pitcher who had those classic World Series battles with Reggie Jackson in the late seventies—the years the Dodgers beat the Phils in the NLCS and moved on to the Series. By 1983, Welch was considered one of the NL's finest pitchers.

"We all knew it was important to win this particular game. We were back at the Vet, and we had that 10ᵗʰ man on our side again. I got three hits in that game plus a walk. I definitely felt in a good groove. I can't explain why. I was seeing the ball well, reading the spin on the ball, and being aggressive at the plate. If anyone ever figures out how to pull that all together every time you step up to the plate, he'll be the greatest hitter in history."

The Sarge's four-RBI performance highlighted a 7–2 win in a game otherwise lacking drama and charm.

SARGE: "I think fans overrate locker room meetings and speeches. None of the veterans on our team ever had to stand up and make a speech or spell out a situation for everybody. We all knew the situation. We were playing at home. We were one game away from winning the NLCS. We had L.A. back on their heels. So we needed to close them out right here at the Vet and avoid playing a Game 5 in L.A.

"Veteran teams don't need a manager for pep talks. They know what they have to do, and they prepare individually for whatever needs to be done. The NLCS series was best-of-five in those days. And we definitely did not want to allow the series to go back to L.A. and have the Dodgers steal a trip to the World Series from us.

"Game 4 was on a Saturday night. The Vet was electric. Everyone in the stands smelled blood. I came up to the plate with Schmitty and Lezcano on base in the bottom of the first. It seemed like Schmitty was on base every time I looked around that series. There was always a little unspoken competition going on between Michael Jack and me. Reuss was on the mound. I knew how Schmitty owned Reuss, so it felt extra good when I was the one who tagged Reuss for a three-run home run in such a big game. I think that dinger iced the series MVP for me because, as I said, Michael Jack had an MVP–type series, too."

Schmidt actually boasted the Phils' highest batting average in that NLCS. He hit a torrid .467, which was followed closely by Matthews' .429. However, the Sarge's eight RBIs and three home runs in four games made him the clear choice for MVP.

J.C.

Snakes. In 2008 and 2009, there were snakes. The Dodgers—the team the Phillies never seem to dodge on the path to a pennant. Unlike the seventies and eighties, the new-century NLCS was a best-of-seven rather than best-of-five affair.

In the 2008 postseason, the national baseball audience witnessed the ascendancy of Cole Hamels, hitherto an enigmatic talent whose potential was sometimes short-circuited by streakiness and a tendency to let adversity get the better of him.

J.C. ROMERO, Phillies pitcher in 2008: "In the NLCS, Cole brought it all together better than any pitcher I ever saw up here. He didn't let anything bother him. Cole was always a quiet kind of guy. When you get to know him, you find he's got a great sense of humor. And he had his head screwed on right for that series. He's a fierce competitor. He saw an important role for himself in the postseason, and he stepped up and filled it."

Cole took the hill for the 2008 NLCS opener. He got off to a shaky start. A Manny Ramirez double in the first scored Andre Ethier, who had also doubled. Carlos Ruiz' passed ball allowed Ramirez to advance to third, but Hamels stopped the bleeding and surrendered a lone run. In the Phils' sixth, Chase Utley and Pat Burrell homered to thrust the Phils into a 3–2 lead that they never relinquished.

J.C. ROMERO: "The only games we seemed to have under control that series were Cole's games. We played some crazy games. But we won! Those crazy games gave me a chance to see a lot of action. It was tough not to get excited in a playoff atmosphere. Philadelphia was electric, and so was L.A."

J.C. posted a 0.00 ERA in both the NLCS and the World Series, winning two games in the World Series. His three wins actually equaled Cole Hamels' postseason win total.

J.C. ROMERO: "Our whole bullpen met the challenge. Myself, I felt strong all postseason. We were all motivated. Our team had come so far.

Cole Hamels pitches against the Dodgers in Game 5 of the NLCS on Wednesday, October 15, 2008, in Los Angeles. *(AP Photo/David J. Phillip)*

We believed in ourselves, and we believed we had the talent to go all the way. All we had to do was go out and prove it!"

Hamels got the win in the first and last game of the NLCS. In between, as J.C. Romero said, it was a free-for-all that the Phils somehow successfully scraped their way through.

In the World Series against the Tampa Bay Rays, it was Cole again who won the opener. Again, the score was 3–2. Again, Chase Utley hit a home run. And again, the Phils lost but one game in the entire series.

J.C. ROMERO: "My second World Series win [Game 5] was pure luck, plus the greatest fielding play I've ever seen! Ryan Madson had given up a homer to Rocco Baldelli and got into a little trouble. They brought me into the game with two outs and Jason Bartlett on second. I located a pitch a little middle-in to [Akinori] Iwamura, and he cracked it up the middle. Chase fielded it. He had no chance to get Iwamura, so he faked Bartlett into thinking he was throwing to first. He threw home and nailed Bartlett and saved my butt and the World Series. Bartlett totally bit on Utley's fake. Chase never had any intention to throw to first. He had no play there."

Utley's amazing play was voted Postseason Play of the Year in the fan voting for *This Year in Baseball.* Cole won the MVP. And J.C.—well…

J.C. ROMERO: "I became an Utley fan for life."

Stairs

MATT STAIRS: "I'm not a very interesting interview. I can't tell you anything exciting about that dinger I hit. I'm sort of a see-ball-hit-ball kind of hitter. I don't over-think when I'm at the plate. All I can tell you is I have the same approach every time I step into the box and that's, 'Swing for the fences.' Look at me: I'm short, I'm chubby. I'm 5'9", and when I had the stick in my hands, I came to realize I should never shortchange myself. I should swing as hard as I could."

Matt Stairs was swinging for the downs when he stepped into the batter's box in the top of the eighth inning on October 13 to face the Dodgers' fireballing Jonathon Broxton. The Phils had entered the inning down 5–3, but a two-run blast by Shane Victorino off Cory Wade knotted the match at 5–5. A subsequent Chooch Ruiz single chased Wade and brought Broxton into the game.

There's a baseball quip sometimes attributed to Joe Hoerner, a Phillies pitcher of long ago. Some claim it was he who first offered, "I swing hard in case I hit the ball." The punch line is now a staple in baseball's trove of initially clever, excessively repeated, and eventually tedious punch lines. But is it possible that it captures the Matt Stairs' approach at bat?

MATT STAIRS: "C'mon, I have a lot more bat control than that. After all, I did knock a few out of the yard in my career."

Matt Stairs launched 265 baseballs out of the playing field in a 19-year career, but none were as important as the one he hit off Broxton. Although a few weeks earlier, Stairs had claimed another "historic" home run.

On September 28, in one of baseball's most compelling individual final-day-of-the-season feats—move over, Roger Maris—Stairs feasted on a Marco Estrada slider and deposited it in the seats. With that homer, Matt became the top home run hitter in the history of baseball among ballplayers who have played for at least 10 different teams. The man he surpassed, Todd Zeile, once played with the Phils. Obviously, he also once played for nine other teams. In fact, there's at least a 30 percent chance that anyone on that particular list played for the Phils. In terms of fatuous records and accomplishments, this particular record rivals the one Tom Selleck's character, Jack Elliot, touts in the film *Mr. Baseball* when Elliot offers that he "led his team in ninth-inning doubles in the month of August."

Matt Stairs had been a Phillie for only one month when he became a hero. The August 30, 2008, trade that brought Stairs to the Phils seemed trifling when it was announced. Stairs came in exchange for Fabio Castro, a 5'7" Dominican portsider who never again appeared in a major league game after the trade. The Phils were seeking some left-handed power off the bench to beef up for the postseason. The 40-year-old Stairs was their answer.

Given Stairs' less-than-ballyhooed arrival in the City of Brotherly Love, no Phillies fan had anticipated what happened when he stepped into the box in L.A. in one of the season's most crucial situations. Stairs simply did his thing. He swung from the heels at a 94-mph Broxton rocket and launched it, as announcer Joe Buck said, "into the night," deep into the right-field seats at Dodger Stadium.

J.C. ROMERO: "We were going crazy for Stairs, yelling, 'la Bomba, la Bomba,' which means 'bomb,' because Stairs hits bombs! The fans didn't see what we saw. We were impressed with him as soon as Matt came to the team, as soon as we saw his power in batting practice."

MATT STAIRS: "It was a big hit all right. You could feel the air go out of that stadium."

J.C. ROMERO: "I think that was the turning point of the series. We knew we were in charge. We were in the driver's seat, and I think Matt's homer took the heart out of the Dodgers."

V

Almost overshadowed by the Stairs round-tripper were Shane Victorino's heroics three batters before. Stairs made history.

MATT STAIRS: "Shane wasn't the most popular guy in L.A. that night. He was their prime target. The L.A. fans were all over him because of a ruckus the night before. I felt happy for Shane when he knocked it out. It set the tone for some good things to come. Fortunately, I got to participate in one of those good things."

The ruckus the day before that Stairs referenced was a Dodgers payback aimed at Shane Victorino. In the second game of the NLCS, Phillies pitcher Brett Myers had chucked a fastball behind Manny Ramirez. The seething Dodgers refrained from retaliating until the time was ripe. It came in Sunday's game when Dodgers hurler Hiroki Kuroda sailed a pitch over Victorino's head.

MARIANO DUNCAN, Phillies 2008 coach: "Victorino is so intense. He had a great postseason against Milwaukee. He hit that big grand slam against CC Sabathia. He was cooling off at this point in the

Shane Victorino hits a two-run home run to tie the game against the Dodgers during the eighth inning in Game 4 of the NLCS on Monday, October 13, 2008, in Los Angeles. *(AP Photo/Chris Carlson)*

NLCS, but the fire in Shane's belly never cools. There was no doubt Kuroda was retaliating. So when Victorino started jawing at Kuroda after he grounded out, our whole team needed to back up Vic. I ran right out to the mound. Next thing I knew, I turned around and everybody was off the bench and running on to the field. I got fined. But I know for sure that after they threw at Victorino's coconut, Vic was going to find some way to make them pay. And he did. His home run was sweet—the best revenge. Anyway, the fight was worth the fine I got. J.C. Romero, Davey Lopes, and Bowa all got fined, too, and I'm sure they were all as happy as me to pay it, too."

Prior to Victorino's eighth-inning heroics, Game 4 of the NLCS was not going well for Shane. He had been the star of the NLDS. His .357 average was second only to Jimmy Rollins' .375. But Shane hit a little slump in the NLCS. By Game 4, his frustration was starting to show. He grounded out and flew out in his first couple of plate appearances. In his third at-bat, he tried unsuccessfully to bunt for a hit. The fourth time proved to be the charm, and Victorino's timing couldn't have been better.

In that at-bat, he was greeted with a lusty chorus of boos. L.A. fans were certain that the game was in the bag. Their super stopper, Broxton, was warming up, prepping for a save in the ninth. *California Dreamin'* blared on the speakers. The PA crew was queuing up Randy Newman's *I Love L.A.,* the song that blares throughout Dodgers Stadium after each victory.

DUNCAN: "Howard had opened the eighth with a single. Cory Wade came in, and Shane came up. I could see the concentration in Shane's eyes. He was locked in. It was like all of a sudden he found his groove again. Wade threw a slider that didn't break. It just kept spinning. Vic didn't miss. He put a perfect swing on it and drove it good. I knew the game was ours at that point. Victorino's hit got us into the Dodgers' heads."

Sweet. Victorino, Victory, Vendetta, V.

chapter 4
Skeletons

Once long ago under founder Billy Penn, Philadelphia could boast a sterling record in terms of class, ethnic, and racial relations. But when Billy Penn's heirs took control, Philly history, frankly, devolved into an unsavory succession of religious, ethnic, gang, and racial clashes. Class warfare.

Yes, in colonial times, the City of Brotherly Love was the most tolerant city of the colonies—a progressive society that did not deign to establish a theocracy that persecuted and excluded all other cults. Under William Penn's 1701 Charter of Privileges, Philadelphia guaranteed religious freedom to all. The Quaker City welcomed not only Quakers but also Lutherans, Anglicans, Presbyterians, Baptists, Mennonites, Catholics, Jews, and dozens of other congregations. Penn explained and proclaimed, "We must give the liberty we seek."

But as the 1950, '83, and '93 Phils can attest, nothing lasts forever. By the early decades of the nineteenth century, Philadelphia had transformed into a testy city beset by class violence among contentious and contending ethnicities, groups, and neighborhoods. The 1844 Nativists riots pitted "natives" (with due apologies to the occupants of preceding millennia) of this continent against nineteenth century Philadelphia's axis of evil—immigrant Irish Catholics.

A revealing aspect of the Nativist Party was their gift for spot-on accurate, albeit unintended, meanings for their own name. The Nativists were also called the Know Nothings owing to members' circle-the-wagons response of "I know nothing," when asked if they had any knowledge about harm that happened to befall non-natives. Nativists didn't give themselves the Know Nothings name, others did, but the nomenclature pleased the Nativists. It conveyed a kind of romantic, menacing vibe of in-but-in-secrecy. Know Nothings' more obvious and pertinent interpretation, which conveyed dumb-as-a-plank stupidity and proud ignorance, escaped them. Though it might have been the first time a thuggish political hate party failed to vet other unintended embarrassing interpretations of its name, it would not be the last.

In the mid-1840s, the Know Nothings were up in arms, literally. Philadelphia's Bishop Kenrick had petitioned the halcyon Philadelphia School Board to permit Catholic students to read the inerrant Douay-Rheims version of the Bible instead of the inerrant King James version during their government-mandated daily Bible reading. The Board gave its okay, which unleashed a righteous measure of Christian-on-Christian crime and violence. The bigger driver of the violence was Protestant Christian fear that the immigrant Irish Catholics—a class, in Nativists view, that was inferior and lacked the Nativists' cultivated tastes—would work cheaper than them and take their jobs. It is shocking that the Nativists would promote the patently un-American notion that the invisible hand of the free market alone should determine which laborers should be hired. But they did.

On May 8, 1844, the Nativists assembled at City Hall and set out with torches, pitchforks, and guns for Kensington where the immigrant Irish population was concentrated. The mob torched the Hibernia Hose Company, St. Michael's Church, St. Charles Borromeo Seminary, and several Irish-Catholic homes. On the way back home, the mob encircled St. Augustine's Church. Ignoring Philadelphia mayor Samuel Rhoads' pleas, the mob set the church ablaze. In the conflagration, the sister bell to Philadelphia's Liberty Bell was destroyed. (Incidentally, Philadelphia, not the federal government, owns the Liberty Bell).

Also destroyed was St. Augustine's brand-new Villanova College, whose first students had just been admitted on September 18, 1843. Villanova was forced to relocate to remote pastures in a tract that in 1890 would become known as the Main Line—named after the new railroad line Pennsylvania Railroad president George Roberts ran through the area. St. Charles Borromeo Seminary was also forced to move because of Nativist terrorism.

Philadelphia's Jacksonian Period (the name history accords the period from roughly the early- to mid-nineteenth century) was far from the pristine and idealized "morning in America" portrait that is often naively portrayed. An unprecedented number of riots and violence marred the era. Violence took the form of ethnic gang fights, fire company rumbles (take the Grim Philly Twilight Tour and get filled in), election day battles, ethnic hostility and fights, violence against blacks, labor violence, owner violence, and vigilante movements.

The era forced Philadelphia and most other major cities to establish police departments that finally quelled the violence and destruction—except for that directed against African Americans, which intensified after the Civil War. Waves of blacks migrating north in search of work and a new life were perceived as threats to jobs, just as the Irish had been in the pre-Civil War era.

That was the state of the city and the nation when the Phillies joined the National League in 1883. Recently freed African Americans were the most marginalized group in a fractionalized society. From the get-go, the owners of the nascent NL clubs held firm to an unspoken rule, ironically termed "A Gentlemen's Agreement," no African Americans could play professional baseball. On January 28, 1901, the American League was founded. Their owners adopted the same rule.

Ben

The retired jersey No. 42 hangs on display at Citizens Bank Park. It sticks out. It's a different color—an irony—from the other red jerseys nearby. The No. 42 jersey is Dodgers blue, not Phillies red. It's a replica of the Brooklyn Dodgers jersey that Jackie Robinson once wore. Since 1997, a replica of Robinson's jersey hangs in every major league park.

The Robinson jersey No. 42 at Citizens Bank Park hearkens back to a confused and confusing era—a time that our country and our city cannot count among its nobler hours. In that era, an entire class of Americans was often legislated out of its right to vote and sundry other rights. African Americans were prohibited from serving in military units with whites. They were refused service at lunch counters and denied admittance to hotels, restaurants, and other public enterprises. Societal mores demanded that they not complain, that they accept a "separate but equal" existence that often effaced them from the American landscape, and that they suffer humiliations in silence, "keep their proper place," and be a "credit to their race."

The world Jackie Robinson faced when he debuted in Major League Baseball was a separate-and-unequal society masquerading and portraying itself as separate but equal. Robinson lived in a nation that billed itself as the land of opportunity, yet willfully limited his opportunities—a land that barred him from earning a job in the sport his nation whimsically called its national pastime.

Jackie Roosevelt Robinson was born in 1919 in Cairo, Georgia, the youngest child of sharecroppers. His middle name, Roosevelt, honored former President Theodore Roosevelt, who died 25 days before Jackie's birth. When Robinson's father abandoned his family, Jackie's mother moved Jackie and his four siblings to Pasadena, California, where she worked odd jobs to support the family. Jackie grew up in relative poverty in a relatively well-to-do community where, from an early age, he felt the sting of exclusion, rejection, and racially based ostracism.

Fortunately, Jackie followed the footsteps of his brothers rather than surrender to the siren call to delinquency. At Pasadena's Muir High School, he starred in baseball, football, basketball, track and—years before Arthur Ashe and the Williams sisters—tennis. Jackie Robinson won the annual Pacific Coast Negro Tennis Tournament in 1936.

Robinson moved on to Pasadena Junior College, starring in track, basketball, football, and baseball, and then he went to UCLA. There he became the school's first athlete to letter in four sports: baseball, basketball, football, and track.

After earning an officer's commission during World War II, Robinson became a Kansas City Monarch in 1945. He endured a farce tryout for the Boston Red Sox that year. The Sox had no intention of signing "a

Negro." The tryout was a smokescreen to schmooze a powerful Jewish Councilman in Boston who was pushing Red Sox GM and Hall of Famer Eddie Collins to evaluate "Negro" talent. The 1945 Red Sox's commitment to that cause seems flimsy when viewed through the prism of history. It wasn't until 1959 that the Red Sox did integrate, and they were the last team in the majors to do so.

One baseball man was serious about integrating, although perhaps he was even more serious about winning. The Brooklyn Dodgers' Branch Rickey dared to smash baseball's Gentlemen's Agreement and field Negro ballplayers. Like today's polemic where business' uncontestable *raison d'être* of generating revenue is disingenuously conflated with the untargeted ancillary happenstance of creating jobs, Rickey's job was to generate wins for Brooklyn's Bums, as Dodgers fans lovingly called their team. Expanding his team's job-applicant pool ahead of the competition seemed to Rickey a business-savvy way to achieve success in the only way success was and is measured: wins.

Rickey knew integrating wouldn't be easy. He handpicked Jackie Robinson because Robinson's education and polish matched his baseball talent. That was the proper combination, Rickey sagely surmised, to overturn baseball's Gentleman's Agreement. Rickey's discussions with Robinson about the travails Jackie would face included, arguably, the most important player-management exchange in baseball history. Rickey admonished Robinson, "You will always have to turn the other cheek." Robinson countered with, "Are you looking for a Negro who's afraid to fight back?" Rickey replied, "I'm looking for a Negro with guts enough *not* to fight back."

That was Rickey's forte—he could close a deal.

The 1947 season opener saw Jackie Robinson at first base for the Dodgers who bested the Boston Braves' Johnny Sain 5–3. Robinson went 0–3 but reached base on an error and scored the winning run.

DEL ENNIS: "Guys on the Dodgers said there was tension in the clubhouse. People seem to think it was just from southerners. It wasn't. They had a few southerners like Dixie Walker and Pee Wee Reese but not many others that I can think of. Where you came from didn't matter. It was mostly about African Americans playing in the major leagues. That was revolutionary then. Younger generations can't imagine how different it was. To people in that era, black baseball players played in their own league—the Negro League, not in the majors. There was a Negro League team in Philly—the Philadelphia Stars. We used to play them occasionally. So did the A's. That's the way it was, and nobody could imagine anything different."

Dodgers star Dixie Walker asked to be traded. Other Dodgers followed suit, albeit cautiously, subordinating principle to pragmatism. Leo Durocher, the Dodgers manager in 1946 who was suspended in '47 but regained the post in '48, recognized Robinson's talent and backed Rickey's program. "I don't care if the guy is yellow, black, or has stripes like a fuckin' zebra. I say Robinson plays. What's more, I say he can make us all rich. And if any of you can't use the money, I'll see that you're all traded."

The Dodgers were 2–2 in the early going when the Phillies moved into Flatbush for a three-game series. It was to be an ugly affair and a blemish on the Philadelphia Phillies.

DEL ENNIS: "Our team had a lot of guys from the South. Andy Seminick was a West Virginian, Skeeter Newsome was from Alabama, Harry Walker was Dixie Walker's brother from Alabama, Putsy Caballero was from Louisiana, Granny Hamner from Virginia, Puddin' Head Jones from South Carolina, Schoolboy Rowe from Texas—but the roughest guy on Jackie Robinson was our manager, Ben Chapman, from Alabama.

"Myself, I was a 22-year-old Philadelphia kid. I was pretty quiet around the vets, but they were brutal on Jackie Robinson that series. Chapman encouraged it. He spent the whole series screaming the 'N' word and 'Snowflake' out as loud as he could, yelling for Robinson to go back to the jungle or back to the cotton fields."

The Dodgers beat the Phils in the first contest. Robinson fisted a single in the eighth, then he kept Phils pitcher Dutch Leonard distracted by drawing several tosses to first before he stole second. The rattled Leonard grooved one to Gene Hermanski, who smacked a single that drove Robinson home for the game's only run.

DEL ENNIS: "The Dodgers swept the series. Robinson didn't do much, but it was easy to see he was a major talent. Chapman could never get himself to admit that. He never let up. He gave nonstop abuse to Robinson, and Robinson had the best possible answer. He won games. The Dodgers swept us three straight. That series set the tone for both of us for the year. They were on the way up. We were on the way down. As for Chapman, he was fired the next year."

Branch Rickey later revealed that Ben Chapman's vitriol "did more than anything to unite the Dodgers." To the city of Philadelphia's credit, In the third game of the Dodgers-Phillies April series, it was a Philadelphian, second baseman Eddie Stanky, who stood up for his teammate Robinson. It was Stanky who held down the second-base spot and forced the rookie Robinson to play first base—a position Robinson had never played before. By the series finale, Stanky had his fill of Chapman. During the course of the game, Stanky suddenly bolted up off the bench. He scrambled up the dugout steps and shouted at the Phillies' dugout, "You son-of-a-bitching cowards! Why don't you pick on someone who can defend himself?"

Jackie Robinson kept his dignity and his cool. It was a struggle. Years later, Robinson wrote, "For a wild and rage-crazed minute I thought, 'To hell with Mr. Rickey's noble experiment. It's clear it won't succeed. What a glorious, cleansing thing it would be to let go.' To hell with the image of the patient black freak I was supposed to create. I could throw down my bat, stride over to the Phillies' dugout, grab one of those white SOB's and smash his teeth in with my clenched black fist. Then I could walk away from it, and I'd never become a sports star. But my son could tell his son someday what his daddy could have been if he hadn't been too much of a man."

The Phillies benefited from the timely flourishing of a group of bonus babies and won the 1950 pennant. They would be the last all-white NL team to do so. Seven years later, they became the last NL team to integrate.

Octavius

Philadelphia played a principal role in what might have been the seminal event that sealed the exclusion of African Americans from organized baseball. The protagonist in the episode was an immensely talented Philadelphia African American, Octavius Catto.

Catto was a black educator, intellectual, and civil rights activist. He was also a star at cricket and baseball. He was reputed to be one of the finer, if not finest, baseball player in nineteenth-century Philadelphia, which was a hotbed of baseball talent.

Octavius was born in South Carolina. His father, William T. Catto, was a freed slave who, after being ordained as a Presbyterian minister, moved his family north (South Carolina not being the most comforting locale for freed black men in antebellum days). Octavius' mother was Sarah Isabella Cain, scion of a prominent, free, mixed-race family named DeReef in Charleston.

When the family came north, Octavius was educated in segregated institutions. As a young activist, he organized 11 regiments of United States Colored Troops in the Philadelphia area during the Civil War. Many were sent to the front and lost their lives there. Catto was also elected corresponding secretary of the Pennsylvania Equal Rights League. He served as vice president of the State Convention of Colored People held in Harrisburg, Pennsylvania. His Philadelphia activism included invoking civil disobedience tactics to desegregate Philadelphia's trolley car system. His tactics succeeded. He achieved his goal.

A worthy precursor to Paul Robeson, Catto was a big sports star. He helped establish Philly as the biggest hub of black baseball in the U.S. In the late 1860s, Philadelphia's African American population was second only to Baltimore's. Catto organized an all–African American team, the Pythians, who elected him their field captain and manager. In 1867, the Pythians traveled to Baltimore, Harrisburg, Camden, and Washington, D.C., for games. Frederick Douglass was in attendance at the D.C. contest, watching his son, Charles, a desk clerk at the Treasury Department, play third base for the Washington club.

Catto believed the baseball diamond provided a non-threatening, neutral platform to win black acceptance into white society. To that end, he scheduled many games against white teams for his Pythians.

The Pythians were successful and exciting. After the 1867 season, the club applied for admission to the Pennsylvania Association of Amateur Base Ball Players. E. Hicks Hayhurst nominated them. Hayhurst was the vice president of the Philadelphia Athletics (a different club from the A's of Connie Mack) and president of the Association's regulating convention. Admission, the Pythians presumed, would be a formality. It was not. For no reason other than racism, the Pythians realized they were going to be rejected. To avoid the anticipated humiliation, they withdrew their application.

Later that year, the National Association of Base Ball Players ruled against admitting any clubs that included black members.

That ruling against a Philadelphia African American team set the precedent for excluding African Americans from baseball—a precedent that prevailed until 1947 when Jackie Robinson made baseball the country's bona fide national pastime.

Octavius Catto played for the Pythians until 1870. He sat out 1871, throwing all his energy into the upcoming election. Class racial violence was brewing again—or still—in Philly. Catto anticipated that local Irish thugs would try to intimidate and bar pro-Republican black voters from voting. Election Day saw black voters in voting lines getting harassed and attacked. Two black men were murdered, shot dead. Late in the day, Catto was also shot. It was established at the time that a man named Frank Kelly killed Catto. Kelly passed Catto on the street, then turned and shot him in the back. The wounded Catto ran for cover behind a streetcar, but Kelly stalked him, caught up to him, and shot him in the heart—dead.

No one was convicted for the assassination.

Octavius Catto's funeral took place on October 16, 1871. Philadelphia city offices and businesses closed out of respect. Contemporary news accounts indicate that thousands of people, black and white, lined Broad Street to pay their last respects. Catto was originally buried at the Mt. Lebanon Cemetery at 17th and Wolfe. His grave now resides at Eden Cemetery in Collingdale, Pennsylvania.

Little Rocked

Richard Anthony Allen had just turned 21 when he headed off to Little Rock, Arkansas. As the most hyped Phillies prospect in over a decade, Dick Allen's future was bright.

LARRY SHENK: former Phillies vice president of public relations: "I started my career here about the same time Dick Allen did. In '61, the Phils were looking for a PR guy. I applied but didn't get the job. They advertised the same position the following year. I applied again. Same result. I figured I could kiss that job goodbye. But a longtime sportswriter, Hal Bodley, encouraged me to toss my hat into the ring the following year. The third time was the charm.

"When I started with the Phillies organization, insiders were really excited about Dick Allen. I had actually seen Allen in action. I grew up in central Pennsylvania and had a chance to watch him play basketball in the state high school championships in Hershey. He was the point guard for Wampum High, which ran the popular controlled offense of that era. That style tied Dick's hands. He wowed everyone with his leaping ability. He was only about 5'10" but could leap 18" above the rim. He was the whole package on the court. He could dribble, shoot, rebound, pass. There's no telling how great he'd have been if he had been freed up to play the wide-open game of today."

MAJE McDONNELL: "The Phils had a scout, John Ogden, who was sky high on Dick Allen. Ogden practically lived with him and his family in high school. Back then before the draft, as I know personally since I was a scout myself, scouts had to be salesmen as much as anything. John was a good salesman. More important, though, he took a sincere personal interest in Dick Allen. He became like a father to him. Dick really trusted John. And the strength and trust of their relationship is why and how Dick Allen became a Phillie."

Ogden signed Allen right out of high school. He reported immediately to Class D Elmira, New York, in 1961 as a naïve 18-year-old. In '62, he graduated to Class C with the Magic Valley Cowboys in Idaho, where he played with two other 19-year-olds who eventually made it to the Philadelphia Phillies: Costen Shockley and Adolfo Phillips. Phillies fans might be shocked that Shockley was the bigger star at Magic Valley. Shockley slammed 23 homers and batted .360 compared to Allen's 21 blasts and .317 average.

In '62, Dick hit .329 in Class A Williamsport. At that point, he hit more for average than power.

MAJE McDONNELL: "Dick blossomed into a power hitter at Little Rock. He started using that big, heavy bat he was famous for. When he started trying to hit the long ball, his average dipped a bit [to .289], but he knocked far more homers [33] than any of his previous seasons. You know, I often thought he changed his hitting style because of the racial stuff he was subjected to in Little Rock."

Nothing in his Wampum upbringing prepared the young Dick Allen for 1963 Little Rock. Only six years before his arrival, Arkansas governor Orval Faubus shamed his religion, his state, and his nation when he dispatched the Arkansas National Guard to block the entrance to Little Rock's Central High School to prevent integration.

Faubus was a huge fan of the minor league team Allen played for—the Travelers. The Travelers were an all-white organization through 1962. They integrated in 1963. Dick Allen was Little Rock's Jackie Robinson.

It's hard to portray—or overstate—the vicious spirit of those troubled times in the Deep South. To make matters worse, almost coincident with the start of the baseball season, Martin Luther King was arrested and jailed in Birmingham, Alabama. There he penned his historic, "Letter from a Birmingham Jail," an enlightened response to eight white Alabama clergymen who grudgingly agreed that while social injustices might exist, the battle against racial segregation should be fought solely in the courts, not in the streets. They castigated King, pinning the dog-whistle tag "outsider" on him and chastising him as having no right to "cause trouble" in the streets of Birmingham.

In Birmingham on May 2, former KKK member "Bull" Connor, Birmingham commissioner of public safety, locked up 959 children aged

Dick Allen, the Phillies' rookie third baseman, in March 1964 at the Florida training camps. *(AP Photo)*

6–18. The next day, he ordered the use of fire hoses and attack dogs. Fire hoses were employed at black citizens for several days. A torrent of denunciations came from around the world until federal intervention stopped the spectacle. The summer of '63 culminated with Martin Luther King's famous march on Washington D.C., and his iconic "I Have a Dream" speech.

Between 1890 and 1968, thousands of towns across the United States drove out their black populations or enacted local legislation to forbid African Americans from living in their towns. The resulting whites-only enclaves were termed "sundown towns" because many of them delineated their city limits with signs typically worded, "Nigger, Don't Let The Sun Go Down On You Here." Alix, Arkansas, a town in Franklin County not too distant from Little Rock, posted that sign as late as 1970.

That was the world in which inexperienced 21-year-old Dick Allen from Wampum, Pennsylvania, found himself. Allen was 1,150 miles away from Philadelphia and did not have the immediacy of support that Jackie Robinson had.

Despite a rocky year at Little Rock, Allen excelled on the diamond. He was far and away the biggest phenom to hit Philadelphia since the days of Roberts and Simmons. Philadelphia fans salivated that 1964 would bring their long-awaited savior.

LARRY SHENK: "I was down to spring training in '64. Dick must've socked 15 homers in Florida. We didn't track spring training stats back then. But he hit some shots I'll never forget. He slammed one into the center-field lights in Tampa that might be the farthest I ever saw a baseball travel.

"When he arrived in Philly, fans expected too much. I'll tell you this, though—he didn't have anything handed to him. Don Hoak, a grisly vet and ex-Marine nicknamed Tiger was the starter at third in '63. He was rough on Dick. Hoak had no intention of losing his job. But, of course, he did lose it.

"Allen won Rookie of the Year in 1964—one year after Pete Rose won. Dick was the All-Star starting third sacker in his sophomore year. He would have made All-Star as a rookie except, in '64, he was competing with possibly the greatest collection of NL third basemen in history. Mathews and Santo—two Hall of Famers—were at or near their peaks. Jim Ray Hart was a Giants rookie. He hit 31 homers. That's more than Allen hit. Ken Boyer, St. Louis' third baseman, was the '64 MVP. And over in the AL, Brooks Robinson, a third baseman and future Hall of Famer, was MVP. But of all of them, Allen was probably considered the greatest natural talent and destined for the biggest things."

Allen's career zoomed out of the gates. He hit .318, drove in 91 runs, and scored 125 runs as a rookie. His average topped .300 in each of his first four seasons. During that stretch, he made the All-Star team three times as a third baseman—twice as a starter.

But Allen became increasingly distant and unhappy after a racially charged brawl with teammate Frank Thomas in '65.

LARRY SHENK: "Dick did have rough sailing after the Thomas incident. He made life interesting for me. It seemed like he was constantly showing up late for team meetings, the team bus, etc. One time, Dick missed a flight to St. Louis. I found that out as I was heading home after a long weekend. I had to turn around, head back to the office, and deal with the media mess.

"I was in the movie theater when Dick pushed his hand through a car headlight. In those days, the only real media was print. There was no Internet, no 24-hour news cycle. Media meant the *Bulletin,* the *Inquirer,* and the *Daily News.* I went to the hospital to see Dick. I came back and explained what happened to the reporters by diagramming on my own hand where Dick's hand was cut. The reporters photographed my diagrammed hand. That's what appeared in the paper the next day."

Dick Allen started printing out messages with his spikes in the dirt cutout around first base. He grew increasingly distant from a team and a city he frankly did not trust. He was shuffled off to St. Louis as part of the historic Curt Flood trade. Allen spent a productive year in St. Louis (34 HR, 101 RBIs) followed by a year in Dodgerland (23 HR, 90 RBIs, .295), before he found his greatest professional happiness and success in Chicago with the White Sox. He won the MVP and led the Junior Circuit in homers, RBIs, walks, On Base Percentage, and Slugging Percentage.

Allen's skills quickly diminished after earning the 1972 MVP Award. Ironically and unexpectedly, he found himself back in Philly to spend the twilight of his career.

LARRY SHENK: "Paul Owens called me into the office one day and asked, 'What would happen if we brought Dick Allen back?' I told him, 'I don't think the fans will accept him.' I was wrong. The fans loved him!"

Allen played first base in 1975 and '76 for the emerging Phils. He batted only .233 and .268, although he did manage to club 15 homers in only 298 at-bats in '76.

LARRY CHRISTENSON, ex-Phillies pitcher: "I remember Dick as a guy who laughed and joked a lot. I couldn't believe all the talk about him being disruptive. And he actually helped me indirectly as a hitter. I used to hit with a big 36" bat that weighed 36 ounces. I broke it one day and had to borrow one of Dick's 43-ouncers. I hit two homers off Mickey Lolich! But then he made me give it back to him. I think he figured the rest of the homers in that bat belonged to him!"

Allen, a free agent, went to Oakland the following year. That's where he ended his career.

Bill James' assessments of Allen highlight the enigmatic nature of his career. James called Allen immature and emotionally unstable. He chose him as baseball's penultimate all-time controversial baseball player, trailing only Rogers Hornsby. However, playing a position teeming with magic/famous/infamous players such as Lou Gehrig, Jimmie Foxx, Hank Greenberg, Willie McCovey, George Sisler, Orlando Cepeda, Mark McGwire, and Albert Pujols—James awards Allen 15th position on his list of all-time best first-sackers.

MIKE TOLLIN, Hollywood producer/director and confidant of Dick Allen: "Dick's career and life were marred by emotional pain, and much of it came from that year in Little Rock. Years after Dick's retirement, I made a film, *Chasing the Dream*, a documentary on Hank Aaron. I showed the film to some kids at a school in Germantown. I took Dick with me. I gave him a big buildup when I introduced him. I told the kids Dick Allen was the only man other than Pete Rose who won both [the] Rookie of the Year and the MVP Award and is not in the Hall of Fame.

"Sadly, the kids didn't know who Dick Allen was, so my intro didn't really connect. But while the movie was on, I noticed Dick had slipped away. I found him standing outside. He said the movie was too painful to watch. He couldn't bear dredging up the memories of those days when he and other African Americans had to endure so much humiliation and pain."

Floodgates

In 1967, Philadelphia once again became the epicenter of an imbroglio with embarrassing racial undertones. This episode transcended a disputed transaction between two baseball clubs. It shook baseball—the industry of baseball—to its foundations.

Thanks to episodes such as those perpetrated by Ben Chapman, Philadelphia had hardly earned a reputation as a city where African Americans dreamed of playing. Dick Allen's sentiment was damning: "I'll play first base. I'll play third base. I'll play the outfield. I'll play anywhere—but Philadelphia."

Curt Flood was a friend of Dick Allen. The two shared their experiences with each other about playing pro baseball as African Americans. Suffice it to say, Dick Allen's account of life in Philadelphia was not a ringing endorsement. So when Curt Flood found out he had been dealt to Philadelphia along with Byron Browne in exchange for Dick Allen, Cookie Rojas, and Jerry Johnson, Flood was livid. His aversion to playing in Philadelphia went far deeper than that of, let's say, J.D. Drew.

Flood was originally signed by the Cincinnati Redlegs in 1956. In the fifties, Cincinnati felt compelled to change its name from the Reds to the Redlegs a few times in order to avoid landing on a McCarthy, Hoover, or Nixon communist-sympathizer watch list. Presumably, no one today questions Cincinnati's loyalty and patriotism, and the team remains the Reds.

Aside from a handful of appearances with the parent club, Flood played almost exclusively in the Redlegs' farm system for two years. He arrived in St. Louis via a lopsided 1957 deal that sent Flood and

Joe Taylor to St. Louis in exchange for Marty Kutyna (who graduated from Philly's North Catholic High School), Willard Schmidt, and Ted Wieand. Only the Philly guy had any kind of career after the trade. Kutyna was 14–16 in a modest career that ended in 1962. Schmidt's career was done by '59, and Wieand pitched a total of 6⅓ innings in MLB. In stark contrast, Flood won seven Gold Gloves. He was a vital cog on the Cards' 1967 World Series championship and the '68 NL pennant-winning squads. Six times for the Cards, he surpassed the .300 mark. On October 7, 1969, when he was traded to the Phillies, the three-time All-Star boasted a .294 lifetime batting average. In 1968, he placed fourth in MVP voting behind three Hall of Famers: teammate Bob Gibson, Pete Rose, and Willie McCovey.

After a superb 1968 season, Curt Flood asked Cardinals owner August "Gussie" Busch for a $30,000 raise. Busch was a throwback to the Gilded Age. He was flummoxed and angered by sixties social movements. Gussie perceived them as ruinous to the country and worse yet, bad for business. In his own business, he was appalled at the liberal direction the Players Association appeared to be shifting toward. Gussie took action. He assembled his property—i.e., the players. He made sure the press was present. And then he complained that the traditional baseball values of loyalty, responsibility, and hard work were eroding, castigating modern players as pampered and overpaid.

The dispirited Cards tumbled into fourth place in a revamped six-team division in 1969. Flood's average tumbled to an uncharacteristic .285, and that "lack of productivity" was the pretext Busch needed to dump Flood, a player Busch viewed as the embodiment of the wrongs of the young generation.

Years later, recounting details of the trade, Flood said he got a call from what he described as a junior official in the Cardinals' front office. Flood balked immediately at the trade. For one reason, the Phillies stunk. For another, Flood was 31. He had already been traded once. He was comfortably settled in St. Louis. He didn't relish the thought of uprooting his family and abandoning the business interests he had established in Missouri. And finally, he was apprehensive about Philly's racist rap. As Flood recalled, "In those days, this country was coming apart at the seams. Good men were dying for America in Southeast Asia and for the Constitution. In the south, we were marching for civil rights. Doctor King was assassinated. We lost the Kennedys. And to think merely because I was a professional baseball player that I could ignore what was going on outside the walls of Busch Stadium was hypocrisy because I found that all those rights that those great Americans were dying for I didn't have in my own profession."

On December 24, 1969, Curt Flood sent a Christmas card of sorts to baseball commissioner Bowie Kuhn. Flood wrote, "After 12 years in the major leagues, I do not feel that I am a piece of property to be bought and sold irrespective of my wishes. I believe that any system that produces that result violates my basic rights as a citizen and is inconsistent with the laws of the U.S. and of the several states. It is my desire to play baseball in 1970, and I am capable of playing. I received a contract from the Philadelphia club, but I believe I have the right to consider offers from other clubs before making any decisions. I therefore request that you make known to all major league clubs my feeling in this matter and advise them of my availability for the 1970 season."

Kuhn's reply was a carefully worded oeuvre of political correctness. It was also an adamant approbation of baseball's hallowed Reserve Clause, which was the essence of the matter. The Reserve Clause had been formally institutionalized in major league baseball since December 6, 1879. Since then, it had been purposefully included in every MLB contract. The clause stated that, upon the contract's expiration, the rights to the player were to be retained by the team to which he had been signed. In practical terms, the clause meant that although both the player's obligation to play for the team and the team's obligation to pay the player were terminated, the player was not free to enter into a contract with any other team.

To Flood's reasoning—and to the reasoning of many others—the reserve clause seemed like legalized slavery. To owners, it seemed like something akin to a covenant not to compete, whose net effect was to enable a cabal among owners to suppress a free labor market. To Curt Flood, a product of the sixties, it meant that a legal system that promises to protect the rights of the individual was not delivering on its promise.

In response, Kuhn wrote, "I certainly agree with you that you, as a human being, are not a piece of property to be bought and sold. That is fundamental to our society and I think obvious."

It was so obvious that Bowie ruled that baseball players were pieces of property that could be bought and sold with no other consideration. In effect, Flood should accept that he is the property of St. Louis, shut his mouth, go to Philadelphia, and take pride that although he is property, at least he is high-priced property.

Flood wasn't about to knuckle under to something he considered an unconstitutional practice. The Players Association led by Marvin Miller backed Flood's cause.

From the outset, Flood said he'd take his case to the Supreme Court. He kept his word. Flood engaged Arthur Goldberg, a former associate justice of the U.S. Supreme Court, as his counsel.

Battle lines were drawn as Charles Feeney and Joe Cronin, presidents of the National and American Leagues, backed Kuhn. They issued a joint statement predicting the end of the world as we know it—or more aptly, the end of the world that best suited them. "Baseball," they warned, "would cease to exist."

As often happens in matters of civil and human rights, Curt Flood became a pariah among his peers—as was Muhammad Ali, recipient of the 2012 Liberty Medal, in the sixties. Flood chastised his fellow ballplayers for their refusal to get involved and back him. He complained that had some big stars publicly taken up the cause, the owners would have backed down. A few notables did go on record as supporting Flood. Bill Veeck, always an outlier, testified on Flood's behalf. So did Hank Greenberg, whose playing career as a Jew had been a constant uphill battle for dignity and rights. And not surprisingly, it was Jackie Robinson who lent the most visible and staunch support.

In the Flood case, the Supreme Court ruled 5–3 in the owners' favor. Curt Flood may have lost his case, but his cause went marching on. The trial bared some weaknesses about the Reserve Clause. Most notably, the Supreme Court conceded that baseball was indeed interstate commerce and the exemption granted to baseball via the ruling was "an anomaly."

Anomalies in law are as unstable as Francium 223. A scant three years after the Flood vs. Kuhn ruling, pitchers Andy Messersmith and Dave McNally again challenged the Reserve Clause. This time, public sentiment was in the players' corner, and the case went to arbitration.

In December 1975, arbitrator Peter Seitz ruled that the Reserve Clause granted a team only one additional year of service from a player—a ruling that, in effect, broke the shackles of the Reserve Clause. For baseball—and other sports—the ruling opened the "Flood" gates to our current era, where ludicrous salaries are commonplace, and owners are richer than Connie Mack could have hoped for in his wildest dreams.

chapter 5

1965

The Year of the Blue Snow. That's what Phillies backup catcher Gus Triandos called 1964. Tons of ink and rivers of Quaker City tears have been shed since 1964 about 1964—but not about 1965. What was the aftermath of the Phils' embarrassment? Was there a morning after, a rebirth, a clearing of the clouds, a Rocky redemption—a something, an anything positive or uplifting in the wake of one of baseball's biggest meltdowns?

Sadly, there was not. In '65, the Phillies accelerated their slide to mediocrity—and into the abyss. They exchanged their all-too-brief status of contending team for that of contentious team.

Donkey

Philly town loves July fireworks. Always has—you can trace that love back to July 2, 1776, the day the Continental Congress voted to declare independence from England. As a brief aside that all Philadelphians should know, July 2, not July 4, was the day John Adams felt should be commemorated and celebrated as "the most memorable Epocha in the History of America," which he penned in a July 3, 1776, letter to his wife, Abigail. But July 4 was selected instead because it was on July 4, 1776, that the Continental Congress, after massive editing and purging, finally approved Thomas Jefferson's text for the Declaration of Independence.

Given the historical gravitas of July 2 and July 4, it's easy to overlook July 3. As it turns out, that's another milestone day in Philadelphia history because July 3, 1965, altered and arrested the course of Philadelphia baseball for the next decade.

After their '64 collapse, the '65 Phillies headed for spring training with promises of redemption, recovery, and reprisal. Instead, they picked up where they left off in '64. They got off to an atrocious start. Entering June, they were in last place. Exiting June, it was a different story. The Phils seemed revitalized and refocused. After an 18–10 June record had zoomed them up to fourth place, a scant 3½ games behind the leader in a tightly contested race, they were suddenly very much in the hunt. As July commenced, they eked out a 4–3 win over Cincinnati. It was their sixth win in a row.

That six-game stretch was destined to be their longest win streak of the year.

On Saturday, July 3, Dick Allen was fielding ground balls at third base during pregame infield practice. Frank Thomas was in the batting cage. Thomas was a power-hitting vet who had joined the Phils via a trade with the Mets in August 1964. As a Met, he had smashed 34 homers in 1962, ranking him sixth in the NL. After Thomas' long-ball production tumbled to 15 in 1963, he became expendable at age 35. For sure, Thomas was a big-time player, although by the time he became a Phil, he was at the end of his career. He had been a three-time All-Star, and despite a career stuck on second-division clubs, he placed among the top 25 in MVP Award voting five times.

The Frank Thomas story included some disturbing personal flaws. He was an old-fashioned hardliner and uncompromising in some of his beliefs. He was a tough guy who liked to prove his grit by betting he could catch anyone's hardest toss barehanded.

JOHN CALLISON: "During infield practice, I stopped by third base to talk with Dick Allen. I started needling Thomas while he was taking his swings in the batting cage. Donkey [as Thomas was nicknamed] had an embarrassing night the night before. With runners on first and third and one out, he tried and failed to bunt three times and struck out. His pride was hurt because Mauch sent him up to bunt. Donkey was still a premier power hitter, even though he was 36 years old. When he missed three bunt attempts, the Phils dugout really rode him. It was pretty much good-natured. Guys were always getting on one another. There's nothing unusual about that. I went over to Dick [Allen] because Donkey was always giving Dick and me the needle. We were two of his favorite targets, so I figured Dick would join in a little good-natured ribbing, too.

"I yelled, 'Hey Donkey!' to Thomas. Don't you know, Thomas swung and missed at a BP toss. Now I had new material, good material, so I yelled, 'Why don't you try bunting?' Thomas kind of ignored me. Instead he shouted at Dick, 'Whatcha tryin' to be? Another Cassius Clay, always mouthin' off?'"

In 1964, Cassius Clay had pulled off what was considered by many boxing aficionados as the greatest upset in boxing history when he defeated Sonny Liston in Miami to become the heavyweight champion of the world. The next day, he changed his name to Muhammad Ali. The white-world establishment was ill-prepared for Ali's decision, but the pent-up rage in the cauldron of the sixties was starting to boil over. Black power and black equality movements had been fraying the nerves of a largely separated and segregated American society. Terms like "Black Power" and "White Backlash" became part of the vernacular.

Thomas was called "Donkey" for a reason. He tended to be stubborn, and his mates confided that he was not the sharpest tool in the shed. Thomas' rookie year was in 1951 when only six of 16 teams in MLB had integrated and when the few African Americans who did play were required to seek lodging separate from their teammates. To Thomas, the wind of change in the sixties was an ill wind that blew no good.

JOHN CALLISON: "Thomas' comments lit Dick Allen up. Things happened fast, but as I remember it, Allen broke toward the batting cage. He threw one left hook and that was it. It decked Thomas. Thomas sprang up swinging his bat. He connected with Allen's left shoulder. At that point, cooler heads prevailed and restored order."

The ugly incident was widely covered and interpreted by many as racially charged.

JOHN CALLISON: "By '64 and '65, there were a number of players of color, like Tony Gonzalez, Tony Taylor, Cookie Rojas, Ruben Amaro, Adolfo Phillips, and others. But there were still only a few African Americans like Wes Covington, Alex Johnson, and John Briggs. Thomas

Buc-Maker

Frank Thomas was a team-shaper, for better or worse—for worse with the Phils, for better with the Pirates. In any event, he did not go silent into that dark night.

When Thomas left Philadelphia in 1965, the Phils, thanks in large part to the Allen-Thomas brawl, were in free fall. When he left Pittsburgh in 1959, thanks indirectly to him, the Pirates ascended to a world championship.

In 1959, Frank Thomas was the key player in a trade that merits consideration as one of baseball's more pivotal, impactful, team-building deals. That year, the Pittsburgh Pirates swapped Frank Thomas, along with the eminently forgettable Whammy Douglas and Jim Pendleton, to the Cincinnati Reds for Harvey Haddix, Smoky Burgess, and Don Hoak.

The deal turned into quite a Buc-maker, helping transform Pittsburgh's Bucs into world champs in 1960. The Bucs couldn't have won it without any of the three players they acquired in the Thomas trade. In 1960, Hoak (who later played for the Phils) placed second in NL MVP Award voting behind the winner, teammate and shortstop Dick Groat. Burgess placed 20th.

In '59, Haddix authored one of baseball's most remarkable feats, twirling 12 perfect innings before losing a heartbreaker in the 13th to the Milwaukee Braves.

In the '60 championship season, Haddix chipped in with 11 regular-season wins, followed up by a World Series–best 2–0 record and a World Series–best 2.45 ERA.

used to do stupid stuff. That's why we called him Donkey. He'd go up to the African Americans and pull their thumbs back, like it was a friendly prank. But they didn't take it that way, and I don't think Donkey meant it to be friendly. It was taken as a taunt because he only did it to them. There was just, I think, an unhealthy amount of taunting in the clubhouse."

In his book, *September Swoon*, Bill Kashatus, a respected baseball historian from Philly, laid a share of the blame for taunting on Allen. In his account, Allen was yelling in at Thomas, "Try to hit one past me." Thomas yelled, "Okay, Richie X, see if you can catch this one." That brought Allen charging into the batting cage, demanding: "You stop calling me Richie X, and I'll stop calling you Donkey."

After Allen returned to third base, Thomas hit a screamer past Allen and yelled, "How'd you miss that one, Richie X?" That was it. Allen rushed the cage again. Punches were thrown. The bat was swung.

The details of the scuffle are murky, inconsistent, and contested. Ultimately, they're not even important. The underlying racial tension that fueled the incident is. Thomas' epithet of Richie X was an irrefutable slap at the Black Muslims, a highly visible, controversial group that was receiving extensive, almost universally unflattering coverage in the media. At the time, the Black Muslims and their charismatic leader, Malcolm X, were a lightning rod for white backlash, fear, and hate.

The Phils lost that July 3 game 10–8. But the loss couldn't be pinned on Donkey or Allen. Allen socked two triples that upped his average to .341. Thomas hit a pinch-hit home run. It was his one and only homer as a '65 Phillie in what turned out to be his final at-bat as a Phillie.

After the scuffle, the Phils put Thomas on waivers. On July 10, he was shipped out to the Houston Astros. There he hit the final three of 286 career home runs. Two years later, his career ended on June 4 after five fruitless plate appearances in a Cubs uniform.

CALLISON: "Donkey got himself fired as soon as he swung a bat at Dick Allen, regardless of whether he was black or white. In baseball, that's a firm rule. You never swing a bat at another player—never."

The incident marked the beginning of the end for Dick Allen's relationship with Philly, as well. Following the incident, all the Phillies, Allen included, were given strict orders *not* to talk about the incident or they would face a heavy fine. However, when the Phillies released Thomas, he gave *his* side of the story to the press and Allen soon found himself cast as the heavy. A popular spin was that a black guy caused a white guy to lose his job.

Pat Corrales, who played for the 1965 team and who managed the Phillies in the early eighties, was quoted as saying that Thomas was a bully known for irritating racial remarks. But for the most part, team members kept mum forever.

These were tumultuous times. Whites were fearful and suspicious about the black social movements of the day. Cassius Clay, a handsome African American, was well liked when he first burst on the public stage. When he suddenly announced he was no longer Cassius Clay and he *demanded* to be called Muhammad Ali henceforth because Cassius Clay was his slave name, many bristled.

Dick Allen's timing couldn't have been less propitious. All his life, he had been called "Dick." Inexplicably, the Philadelphia press had insisted on calling him "Richie." Allen's requests to be called "Dick" rather than "Richie" were conflated with Ali's change of name and a contemporary wave of other African American name changes.

The Phillies tanked quickly after that incident. They went from a contending team playing at a .655 clip for the preceding month and picking up steam to also-rans barely playing .500. Much if not most of the blame was laid on Allen. The boobirds booed with more gusto. There's nothing unusual about that in Philly. Ask Del Ennis or Mike Schmidt. The difference in Allen's case was that the booing expressed something more insidious than performance on the field of play.

By season's end, the Phillies had become irrelevant. They would remain so for years to come.

Art

CALLISON: "When you play baseball as long as I did, you see so many things that it's impossible *not* to forget a ton of what you saw! Fans approach me every day, asking if I remember this game or that play. Their memories amaze me! They remember things I did that I can't recollect at all. But one thing I remember vividly was Art Mahaffey's debut. It was a treat to watch.

"It was back in late July in '60 when Art came up. We were playing the Cards and losing. We were in last place or near last. And we were already hopelessly out of the race. Ah, those days were tough. It was especially tough on me because I had played on a pennant winner in '59 with the White Sox. When I came to the Phils, I found an entirely different mentality. These guys were used to losing, and they accepted it. But Mauch was changing things. I could see that right away. Still, we didn't have much to cheer about that season, so Art's debut was a breath of fresh air.

"Art came into the game in the [seventh] and struck out Ken Boyer and somebody else [Darryl Spencer]. The only guy he didn't strike out was John Glenn. Guess why I remember John Glenn! He was only in the majors for a cup of coffee in '60. Then he was gone forever. Next time I heard the John Glenn name was in February of '62! He was America's first astronaut! We joked a lot about that one in the clubhouse! You know, like, 'Hey, life after baseball can be great. Look what John Glenn's doing!'

"Art's first inning was impressive, but lots of guys have struck people out in their debut. The treat came in Art's second inning. Bill White, a tough left-handed hitter who later played for the Phils, singled. Now remember that Art Mahaffey was a righty. But he proceeded to pick off Bill White. Bill White is *not* a base-stealer. He was only a step off first base. But Art's move is so deceptive that he nailed White by a mile! I can still see White's face! He couldn't believe what just happened!

"Next, Curt Flood singled. And what do you know! Art caught him napping, too. I don't think anyone had ever seen a right hander with such a deadly pickoff move. I know I hadn't. Art had the best right-handed move I ever saw. It might have been the best move, period."

ART MAHAFFEY: "As a kid growing up in Cincinnati, I always dreamed of playing in the big leagues. I always worked on my pickoff move. Picking runners off probably gave me a bigger kick than anything else. I always predicted that if I ever pitched in the majors, I was going to pick off the first two guys that got to first. I kept my word, and I got to see how Philly fans react when they like your performance."

Mo'

When asked what he was going to do after the 1964 apocalypse, Johnny Callison replied, "The first thing I'm going to do is find a place to hide."

CALLISON: "I really think the Phillies were primed to succeed in 1965. We were optimistic. Things just didn't go our way. Luck plays into everything in baseball—hits, bounces, pitches, umpire's calls, everything. I think our '65 lineup was stronger than '64. We made some good changes. I don't know if Mauch and the front office purposely made changes so everyone in the whole clubhouse wasn't carrying the '64 monkey on their backs. But infusing some new blood helped the team to forget. We added first baseman Dick Stuart, Dr. Strangeglove as they called him. Dick wasn't the best guy handling throws in the dirt or catching foul pops, either. But he had tremendous power and hit 28 homers for us in '65.

"I don't think Mauch ever appreciated Stuart. He liked Stuart's clout, but Stu's fielding drove Mauch crazy. Cookie Rojas took over second base from Tony Taylor, and Cookie hit over .300 for us. Ray Culp started to emerge. He had a good year. What really hurt us was that Art Mahaffey had arm trouble. He was always good for a dozen or so wins and he only won a couple in '65. He was out of baseball a year or two later. What a shame. Art could battle out there on the mound, but injuries cut his career short."

The Phils won their opener in '65, defeating the Houston Astros 2–0 in Houston on a Chris Short shutout. They returned for a six-game home stand, and a few days later, after a 13-inning 2–1 victory again over Houston the Fightins climbed up to second place. It lasted only one day. It was to be their highest climb of the season.

CLAY DALRYMPLE: "Mauch had a solid philosophy—beat up on the bad teams. That's what carried us in 1964. We had great records against the second-division teams. [The Phils were 13–5 versus Houston and 15–3 versus the Mets in 1964.] If you take those games off of our overall record, I'll bet we weren't much better than .500. [Subtracting the results of Mets and Colt 45s games results in a record of 64–62, one decision removed from .500.] In '65, we didn't dominate the bad teams to the same extent, and that impacted our record a lot."

CALLISON: "Personally, I got off to a terrible start. I was hitting about .185 in May. Slumps used to really upset me. They made me moody and preoccupied. I always took things too hard, and it affected my performance—to say nothing of giving me the ulcer I wound up with. You know what I did to battle my depression? I started doodling in my kids' coloring books. I went out and bought some art books and started doing those paint-by-number kits. You know, 'Color 1 red, color 2 blue, color 3 green.' I used to joke that the only problem with that was that saying 1-2-3 kept reminding me what my batting average was."

By May 1965, the 20–24 Phils were in next-to-last place, already eight games behind the leader. Their two aces were coming up short. Short was 4–6, Bunning 4–4. Both had ERAs near 4.00. But an 18–10 surge in the month of June lifted the team into fourth place, only 5½ games behind.

However, from July through the end of September, discounting three meaningless games to end the season, the Phils were only two games better than .500—hardly the stuff of pennant winners.

JACK BALDSCHUN: "Things didn't go our way in '65. It seemed like we were always behind and playing catch-up. In '64, it seemed like we were always ahead. And in the standings, it was the same. We started off in first in '64 and kept going. In '65 we started behind and were never successful catching up."

CALLISON: "It seemed like whenever we got into a winning rhythm, we ran into Bob Gibson, Sandy Koufax, Don Drysdale, or Juan Marichal. There were a lot of aces in the NL in that era. We had two of them: Bunning and Short. Fortunately, we didn't have to face either of them!"

Despite their subpar starts, when the season ended, Short (18–11, 2.82) and Bunning (19–9, 2.60) were right where you'd expect them to be. But their contributions weren't nearly enough.

CALLISON: "That slow start hurt us mentally. It was too similar to the end of '64. It's not that we accepted losing. I really don't think we ever had that mentality and, if there had been any sign of that, Mauch would have gone through the roof! But baseball is a game of rhythm and momentum. We had momentum from Day 1 in 1964 until Day 152. Then the momentum turned on us and, unfortunately, I think we carried it forward into 1965."

Art went on to become the Phils stopper through a couple of their leanest years. He was his team's lone All-Star. On April 23, 1961, he fanned 17 Cubs in nine innings. In '65, his pitching mate, Chris Short, surpassed him for most Ks in a game when Shorty whiffed 18 Mets. But it took Shorty 15 innings to rack up that many.

ART MAHAFFEY: "It's a different game now. Pitchers used to pitch nine innings, even extra innings in my day. Remember Harvey Haddix's 12-inning perfect game? Today, they'd have yanked him in the seventh or eighth based on pitch count. In Haddix's day, a manager took his life in his hands if he tried to yank a guy out early. Pitch counts didn't exist. Starting pitchers wanted to finish their games because if we didn't finish, it put our job in jeopardy. In '64 I pitched 8⅔ innings one night. Somebody hit a bloop single to right. Mauch pulled me out of the game. The reliever—I think it was Baldschun—got the next guy out. The next day, when I walked into the clubhouse, Stan Hochman, Ray Kelly, and some other sportswriters were sitting around. They didn't say a word to me. Finally I said, 'Why didn't you guys say, "Nice game" to me last night?' One of them answered, 'You didn't really win. You didn't finish!'

"Could you imagine that today? Pitchers get kudos for 'quality starts' for pitching games that, had you pitched the same game in my era, you'd be reading bad stuff about yourself in the paper next day. Back then, it wasn't a good game unless you finished it yourself."

When Mahaffey was healthy, he finished his games. In 1961, he finished ninth in the NL in complete games. In 1962, he was tied for second with Billy O'Dell behind future Hall of Famer Warren Spahn for the NL lead in complete games. Mahaffey also knows about strikeouts. Despite a career curtailed by injuries, Art ranks 11th on the Phillies' all-time list of games with 10 or more strikeouts. Art pitched six. The guys directly ahead of him on the list each recorded seven. Their names are Robin Roberts, Roy Halladay, and Robert Persons—impressive company.

Unfortunately, 1965 was the year of Art's demise. From a productive 12-win '64 season, Art slipped to 2–5, 6.21 in '65. That fall-off just might account for why the '65 Phils didn't contend. In '65, when the Phils lost

Mahaffey as a solid No. 3 pitcher behind a Hall of Famer (Bunning) and an All-Star (Chris Short), their goose was cooked. Toss in the 10-win difference between Mahaffey's 12 wins in '64 and two wins in '65, and the '65 Phils win 95 games—five more than in 1964. In other words, the '65 Phils would have contended for or won the pennant.

MAHAFFEY: "My arm was in bad shape by 1965. I pitched in pain throughout my career. Pitchers back then were panicked about arm trouble. Clubs would send you down to the minors if you had a sore arm. And we knew that when they did, they'd bring up the next hard-throwing kid and throw his arm out. Arm trouble was hanging constantly over our heads.

"We didn't have enough starting pitching in '65. Whether that lost the pennant for us or not, I don't know. Bunning won 19, Short won 18, and Ray Culp won 14. But that was it. No other starter won more than [five]. Bo Belinsky had a number of starts but only a couple of wins. We traded for Lew Burdette and Ray Herbert, a couple of guys who had some great years previously. But their great years were behind them. Both of them retired within a year or so. Had I not been injured and chipped in with a dozen or so wins, who knows?

"But I did have arm trouble, and with good conditioning I could have avoided it. I laugh at the 'prevailing wisdom' in baseball during my playing days. They knew nothing about conditioning. And what they did know was not only wrong but often harmful. Pitchers were told not to lift anything more than three pounds. They were sure that weight training ruined a pitcher's arm. They actually cautioned us that the arm could pull out of the shoulder socket. Steve Carlton changed that old-line thinking. His workouts—and his success and longevity—disproved those old notions. After my playing career, I started working with a Nautilus machine. I really got into physical fitness. I believe that I might have pitched 15 more years if I could have worked out like that as a player.

"My arm troubles actually started a few years earlier. I pitched one cold, windy night with the temperatures in the mid-40s. I went nine innings and won 2–1. Afterward, my arm felt sore. Then I started seven of our next 20 games. My arm got progressively worse. I was afraid to say anything for fear of being sent down. Sounds strange to fans nowadays, but that's the way pitchers felt. Pitch in pain, and keep your mouth shut. Plus, I was the ace of the staff in those years and felt I had an obligation to keep pitching."

Mahaffey was a key member of the '64 staff, too. He was the No. 3 right behind Bunning and Short in the rotation. Dennis Bennett was the other guy in a four-man rotation. Bennett had a good year in '64. In fact, Bennett and Mahaffey were the protagonists in four of the five 1–0 games that the '64 Phils played. Bennett came out on top in two of them, and Mahaffey suffered losses in two. I mention those 1–0 games because one of them is considered the precipitating event of the '64 collapse.

MAHAFFEY: "The game was 0–0 in the sixth. I got the first guy out. Then Chico Ruiz, a Cincinnati rookie, singled to right. The next guy, Vada Pinson—maybe the fastest player in baseball at the time—singled to right and tried to stretch it to a double. Johnny Callison out in right gunned him down. What a gun! I believe Johnny's arm ranked right up there with Clemente's. Then up stepped Frank Robinson, one of the game's finest hitters who was fantastic in the clutch. What happens? Ruiz steals home—right out of the blue. He would have been buried in the minors forever if he was out! But he wasn't, and that started our 10-game slide. We lost the next nine in a row."

No matter how you analyze it, the loss of Art Mahaffey played prominently in the disappointment that was the 1965 season—the gonna-do-it-this-time-around season that never unfolded.

Dalrymple

Clay Dalrymple is not the guy you'd expect to see at a Hollywood casting call. No offense to Clay, but let's say his looks were more rugged than Hollywood handsome. Notwithstanding, Dalrymple enjoys a pervasive presence on both the silver screen and TV. Watch a movie produced or directed by Mike Tollin, and you'll likely see a character named "Dalrymple" sometime during the show.

MIKE TOLLIN: "It's my little, sneaked-in, wink-and-a-nod homage to Clay Dalrymple, because he was my favorite Phillie when I was growing up. You know how it is with kids—especially Delaware Valley kids! Everybody winds up picking a favorite player. Then you live and die with him each day, scouring the box score to see how he did. Clay Dalrymple was my favorite. Why Dalrymple? I have no idea. That's the beauty of being a young fan. There doesn't have to be a reason."

Mike is a Main Line expatriate whose zip code is now 90210. His change in latitude brought no change in attitude. He's still fiercely loyal to the Phils. What's more, it's not only Mike who's a Phillies fan. So are his kids. Mike raised them with proper Philly "values."

TOLLIN: "When my kids used to go out for Halloween, the neighbors didn't have to guess too hard who the Tollin kids were. They were the ones wearing Phillies uniforms. I'm serious. That's how they dressed for trick-or-treat. I got a kick out of sending them out in to the heart of Dodgerland dressed as Phillies. And honest, it wasn't my idea. My five-year-old came up with it. He demanded to dress up as Jim Thome."

The whole Tollin family is onboard the Phillies train. But it took a little coaxing.

TOLLIN: "When I first moved to L.A., I told my then-fianceé, 'There's something you need to know if you're going to marry me.' She got a little anxious, bracing herself for something deep or dark. She was surprised and I guess relieved when I said, 'Look, honey. You're marrying a rabid Phillies fan. My only demand going into this thing is that we *must* raise our kids as Phillies fans, not Dodgers fans. If you have problems with that, we'd better call it off now.'"

Robbie (Roberta Rowe) is now Mike's wife. Perhaps her name, Robbie, was part of the attraction for Mike, given that one of the Phillie Nation's most revered names is Robbie, as in Robin Roberts. Just sayin'.

TOLLIN: "Yeah, my wife's onboard with the Phils. We're so rabid, she pretty much had to come over to the Phillies side, especially when she heard our son Lucas' first words, which were, 'Outta here!' Harry Kalas' classic home run call."

Howard

Howard Cosell blustered into sports broadcasting in the mid-1950s. For better or worse, Cosell, controversial and contentious, reinvented the sports interview. His style was abrasive, arrogant, and unrepentant. He bullied sports personalities, brandishing high-and-tight questions at athletes who had never had to swing at anything but softballs lobbed into their wheelhouse. Brutishly, Cosell would often try to embarrass, confuse, and humiliate interviewees by employing a lexicon beyond their ken.

He stopped at nothing in his efforts to provoke the most outrageous story, the most over-the-top reaction, or the most regrettable comment from his too frequently overmatched quarry.

So, as MLB headed down to Florida for 1965 spring training, when Howard Cosell's front men approached Gene Mauch with the request that Cosell interview him, Mauch emphatically refused. Initially.

JOHN CALLISON: "Mauch told me this story during spring training that year. Mauch probably didn't sleep a single night from the last out in '64 until spring training. He was itching to get back and redeem himself and the team. Nobody could mention anything about 1964 to him. It was a dead issue. He wanted the players to focus on the '65 season, not the previous one. He didn't want us to lose faith in ourselves. And he didn't

When Mike got out of college, he landed a job with MLB Productions. He did a ton of work with the Phillies' video department and produced the 1980 World Champions Phillies highlight film as well as *Centennial—100 Years of Phillies Baseball*. In the mid-80s, he did *Phanatic Phillies* featuring Tug McGraw and the Phillie Phanatic followed by *Whatever It Takes, Dude,* the ode to the 1993 squad narrated by Lenny Dykstra.

Mike went on to direct and produce several TV shows and movies such as *Radio, The Zookeeper's Wife, Summer Catch, Coach Carter,* and *The Perfect Score.* Two of his successful shows were *Arli$$* and *Smallville.* At this writing, he has 51 titles credited to him. But through it all, he has want the press to play that whole nightmare out again. Mauch wasn't fond of the press to begin with."

After Mauch refused the interview, Cosell himself called Mauch. He kept hounding Mauch, who insisted, "I'm not talking to anybody about 1964, least of all you, Mr. Cosell. I've seen the circus act you do with Muhammad Ali, and I'm not putting myself or my men through that humiliation."

Cosell provoked many highly publicized verbal sparring bouts with Ali. Although Cosell didn't fare much better in those contests than he would in the actual ring, Mauch didn't want to match wits.

Cosell tried a new tack. He gave Mauch his word he wouldn't say a word about 1964. Given that assurance, Mauch relented. He agreed to an interview.

CALLISON: "Right after Mauch returned to Clearwater and set up shop in the Phillies' Jack Russell Stadium, Howard Cosell and his entourage came to town. Mauch told me the camera crews came into his office, set up the lighting, checked the sound, and got everything prepped for Cosell. At that point, Cosell waltzed in and sat down. The cameras started to roll, and the very first words out of Cosell's mouth were, 'Gene, how did it feel to blow a 6½ game lead with 12 games left to play last season?'

Mauch, true to his word and true to form, bolted upright and flew out of the room with a hearty, 'Fuck you, Cosell.'"

remained true to his roots. In fact, if you check him out on the IMDB website, you'll read only one succinct clip as his biography: "Philadelphia native and a lifelong Philadelphia sports fan especially a fan of the Philadelphia Phillies."

Mike Tollin has not forsaken his hometown. Nor has he forsaken his boyhood Phillies idol, Clay Dalrymple, the mostly forgotten backstop on the '64 Phils.

TOLLIN: "Yes, you'll find 'Dalrymple' characters in various *ARLI$$* episodes. In *Summer Catch*, you'll find a character named Miles Dalrymple and, well, I sort of sneak a Dalrymple in every chance I get. Everybody on the set is on to that little trick."

Is Clay Dalrymple aware of his immortalization?

CLAY DALRYMPLE: "I had no idea! It's flattering. I don't want to disappoint Mike Tollin, but I don't really know any of those films. I'm sure they were big hits, but I live up here in Golden Beach, Oregon. We're remote and out of touch. I like it that way. The nearest town is 27 miles away. You know why it's 27 miles away? That's the number of miles a stagecoach could travel in a day. That's how they figured out where to situate towns. There's another ball player that lives nearby: Hall of Famer, Bobby Doerr. He lives one town—one stagecoach stop—away from Golden Beach."

I asked Clay Dalrymple for his thoughts on what happened in 1965. Why did his team simply drop out of sight?

CLAY DALRYMPLE: "It's nice to be asked about 1965! I'm tired of talking about 1964.

"After '64, I don't think our guys had to endure the kind of stuff Bill Buckner went through in Boston. I think Philadelphia still warmed up to us after our collapse. And it was a collapse. I can't give you any reason why it happened. We didn't choke, I'm sure of that. It was just a stretch where nothing went our way, and the stretch came at the worst possible time. Those slumps happen in baseball, and I have no explanation why.

"As for 1965, I *can* tell you a little about that. We were a good team—even a little better than the '64 squad—not much better, but a little better. I always thought we could compete. The '65 Giants had a scary lineup with Mays and McCovey, but Cepeda missed practically the whole '65 season. That made San Francisco more beatable. They also had Juan Marichal, one of baseball's greatest pitchers, and Gaylord Perry. Then there were the Dodgers. They had virtually no punch in their lineup. They had amazing pitchers with Koufax, Drysdale, Osteen, and Podres. But we had Bunning and Short. And our lineup—well, we had a better starting eight than the Dodgers. I felt we were stronger than the Pirates who had Stargell and Clemente. But we had Callison and Allen whose numbers compared very well with almost anyone's. So yeah, we had the horses to compete.

"I think we did have some negative carryover from '64 in terms of not fully believing in ourselves. Mauch didn't let us get intimidated. He was good for us in that way. But we lost big when Art Mahaffey got injured. That's a hole we never filled. And the incident with Dick Allen—I don't think we recovered. We went on a skid after that. Things changed around the clubhouse. Things changed with the fans. Allen started getting boos, and it affected him on and off the field.

"Another thing that hurt in '65 was getting off to a bad start. Emotionally, on the heels of 1964, we needed a good start. When it didn't happen, it had an effect, and the effect wasn't good. We really came to camp that year ready to make up for '64. The slow start kind of took the wind out of our sails."

As for Clay Dalrymple personally, his career tailed off precipitously after '64. He lasted six more years, but with the exception of his .245 average in 1966, Clay's average was generally south of .220.

DALRYPMLE: "I had decent numbers as a rookie in '60. I hit .272. I slipped the following year but bounced back in '62. I thought I had come into my own. I hit 11 homers and had a .276 average again. In '63, I hit 10 homers, but my average dipped a bit. And then, for some reason, I developed a hitch in my swing. I never figured it out. I never could correct it. I never again put up numbers like I did those first few years when I looked promising. I just stopped hitting."

chapter 6

Lefties

The Phillies had their first great left-handed pitcher in the early part of the twentieth century when lefty Eppa Rixey and Grover Cleveland Alexander partnered in a lefty-righty, future–Hall of Fame tandem that led the Phils to their first pennant in 1915. Alexander won 31 games that year. Rixey chipped in with 11. The two accounted for 47 percent of the Phils' 90 victories. In 1918 Alexander was traded to the Cubs. Rixey last donned Phillies flannels in 1920. With Alexander gone, it's no surprise the Phils sunk to last place by 1919. With Rixey gone the next year, it's also no surprise they remained in last or next-to-last place for the remainder of the twenties.

After Rixey, the Phils had nothing but forgettable portsiders. But starting around 1950, the Phils started a skein of great and near-great left-handers—a quartet whose only common denominator was great stuff on the mound. Off the mound, their denominators were neither common nor commonplace.

The Egyptian

CURT SIMMONS, Phillies star left-hander 1947–50, 1952–60: "I didn't do much to help the sale of lawnmowers!"

Curt Simmons is joking about an accident he had around his house in the fifties. This may shock current ballplayers, but Curt actually cut his own lawn with a power lawnmower he didn't sit on but pushed by hand. Simmons pitched in an era when ballplayers could often be caught performing menial tasks in their modest but pleasant neighborhoods.

SIMMONS: "Yeah, I got a little sloppy and nipped off the toe. The injury set me back a bit, I think."

It didn't set him back too much, if you check his accomplishments. Curt was one of the NL's top lefties in the fifties. In fact, Simmons was arguably the decade's finest NL lefty behind Hall of Famer Warren Spahn. Simmons was also one of the Carpenter family's first big-ticket bonus signings.

ROBIN ROBERTS, Phillies Hall of Fame right-handed pitcher and stablemate of Simmons: "Curt got the most bonus money among the Whiz Kids. I got $25,000 to sign. That was great money in those days—more than I had ever seen. There's no doubt about it, the bonus money was the reason I became a Phillie. I wasn't a Phillies fan. I grew up in Springfield, Illinois. That was Cubs and White Sox territory. I was a Cubs fan as a youngster.

"After high school, I went to Michigan State University where I played baseball. I played basketball there, too. At that point, I favored basketball over baseball, but the NBA didn't exist yet. [The NBA was founded in 1946.] Besides, at that time and for all my young life, the country was more interested in baseball than any other pro sport. Pro football wasn't as big nationally as college football. My alma mater, Michigan State, attracted crowds for football games that were way bigger than any crowds the Detroit Lions drew.

"As I said, growing up, I mostly followed the White Sox and the Cubs. I probably would have been happy playing for them, too. But they didn't offer money like the Phils did, so I went with Philadelphia's offer. I never had any regrets. Philadelphia was wonderful to me. But, getting back to Curt, he got a $65,000 signing bonus. That was really a tidy sum in the war years!"

Jackie Donnelly, the Phils' groundskeeper in the forties and fifties told me a story years ago. "The Phils went all out to get Curt. Curt grew up in Egypt, Pennsylvania, a little town not very far from Philadelphia. It was close to Bethlehem—up in Chuck Bednarik territory, not far from Lehigh University. There was an old joke among the people in that area that people wanted to get out of Bethlehem so badly that they 'fled' to Egypt.

"Curt was a local superstar for Whitehall High School. The Phils were high on him. I believe that 15 of the 16 MLB teams were all in a bidding war to sign him. The Phils pulled out all the stops. In order to impress Curt and the local townsfolk, they scheduled an exhibition game against Curt and his high school team. It had to be the biggest day in the history of little Egypt, Pennsylvania.

"You're not going to believe this, but Curt and his high school team almost beat the Phils! Curt threw as hard as major leaguers in those days, particularly since most of the top players were away fighting in World War II. He told me once that one of his outfielders misjudged a ball, and it cost him the game. After the game, the Phils joined the whole town back at the high school for a barbeque."

Perhaps it was the barbeque that tilted Curt's decision in the Phillies' direction. In any event, he signed and went on to a great professional career. Simmons debuted on September 28, 1947, with a nifty 3–1 victory over the New York Giants.

"I went the distance," Curt recalled. "I had a shutout for eight innings. Buddy Blattner singled a run home in the ninth, but I wasn't really in trouble. What a feeling that was! The Giants had a lot of stars like Johnny Mize, the Big Cat, who eventually made it into the Hall of Fame. Bobby Thomson, the guy who hit The Shot Heard Round the World, was in the lineup that day. For our part, the Phillies finished seventh that season, but we were very young. We had Del Ennis, Granny Hamner, Willie Jones, and Andy Seminick in the lineup the day I debuted. Those guys were going to be heard from in baseball. You could tell."

After his promising debut, things got a little rocky for the lefty whose unique, deceptive, herky-jerky pitching windup was his trademark.

SIMMONS: "That was my first and only major league appearance in 1947. The next year, I was up with the Phils for good. Things were changing rapidly in baseball that year, just like they were nationally. Our servicemen were back stateside or headed back soon. As the top players returned, the quality of competition went up quite a bit. Plus, Jackie

Robinson had broken the color barrier in 1947. He was a great player, and he opened the door for a lot of other fine players.

"Baseball and professional sports in general were getting more and more popular. More people were showing up at the ballpark. But in 1948, the A's were still outdrawing us in Philadelphia. Historically, the A's always outdrew the Phillies. Anyway, the A's finished over .500 in '48 and made it into the first division. We finished [sixth] in the standings and last in attendance."

Baseball people of the era said that Philadelphia, which was suffering an extended period of industrial decline, was no longer a two-franchise town. As matters turned out, the Phillies, who were historically the city's weak sister baseball franchise, found success at the right time. A Philadelphia Phillies franchise that was spending money for the first time, coupled with a successful youth movement, fired up Philadelphians. In '50, the Phils got hot as the A's tanked. The Phils significantly outdrew the A's, which put the A's deeper into the financial hole, sowing the seeds for the A's departure from Philadelphia.

SIMMONS: "I had my first taste of losing in 1948. That season my first manager, Ben Chapman, got fired. We set some kind of a baseball record, I think, when our trainer, Dusty Cooke, took over the team. I don't follow these things, but I think Dusty might be the only trainer who ever managed a professional baseball team. Dusty only had the job a couple of weeks before they brought in Eddie Sawyer. With all those changes, and the team not playing well, I went 7–13. That losing record took some getting used to. I had always been a winner! Not too long after that, the Phils and I started getting things right. In our 1950 pennant-winning season, I more than reversed that losing record and went 17–8. Then I pretty much stayed on the right side of .500 for the rest of my career."

Despite pitching in some pretty lean years, Curt ended up an impressive 115–110 with a 3.66 ERA in 13 years with the Phillies. He was traded to the Cards in 1960 where he went 7–4, 2.66 in his first season. A few years later at age 35, Curt was a mainstay on the '64 Cards staff.

That's the year, ironically, that the Cards overcame a huge Phillies' lead and won the NL flag.

Simmons ended his 20-year career in 1967, amassing a sterling 193–183, 3.54 slate—all the more impressive considering the time he lost to military duty at the peak of his talent. Like the rest of the lefty foursome in the chapter, Curt never twirled a no-hitter. But he came closer than any of the other lefties here. He came close not only to a no-hitter but to a perfect game.

SIMMONS: "How could I forget that game! By 1953, I'd have to say I was pretty much established and respected as a pitcher. I had started the '52 All-Star Game. I made the All-Star roster in '53, too. But this particular game came before All-Star break. I threw a one-hitter, and that one hit was by the leadoff batter, Bill Bruton, in the first inning. What a ballplayer Bruton was! He's not remembered much because he played in the finest group of center fielders I can imagine. We had Richie Ashburn, the Giants had Willie Mays, the Dodgers had the Duke Snider, the Reds had Gus Bell. I think Stan Musial played center that year for the Cards. And the Braves had Billy Bruton. I just wish they didn't have him *that* day!"

Curt's right. That center field contingent was formidable. And he left another decent one off the list: Frank Baumholtz of the Cubs batted .307 in 1953.

SIMMONS: "The Braves had just moved from Boston to Milwaukee, and the fans were crazy for that team, and the Braves were killing every other team in baseball attendance-wise. They cheered every fly ball as if Ruth had just crushed one.

"Bruton hit my very first pitch for a single up the middle. He told me later he was sitting on a fastball, and I gave him one he could handle. Otherwise, my location was perfect. I beat a pitcher named Don Liddle whose career was short, but who had a few good seasons [Liddle's career line was 28–18, 3.75].

"That Milwaukee team was very good. They were led by Eddie Mathews, who had his best season that year. He was on the first cover of

Sports Illustrated. They also had Joe Adcock, Del Crandall, Andy Pafko, Johnny Logan—the nucleus of the team that won a couple of pennants a few years later. They became the team to beat after Hank Aaron came on board the following year. I'm glad I didn't face him that day. Those 27 consecutive outs would have been a lot tougher to get.

"As it stood, I struck out 11 and didn't walk anyone. I had great command—and even though we were a good fielding team, the Braves didn't really hit anything that required a great fielding play.

"I still have the ball from that game. Stan Lopata, our catcher, used to fix up balls for us after special games. He'd mark date and score on it and add something like, 'Curt had trouble today, but he battled hard'—something like that. Stosh was a would-be artist, so he always drew something on the ball, too. I've given a lot of those balls away over the years, but not that ball, the one from my almost-no-no game—well, that one stays for the grandkids."

Style

The Phils' 1964 club's 25-year reunion was a festive occasion. Much of the sting of that embarrassing campaign was gone by 1989, but a lot lingered. Tall tales flowed in direct proportion to the consumption of wine and beer. Sadly, a sense of dread haunted the festivities more visceral and elemental than a botched baseball season. Pitching great Chris Short was lying in a coma in a hospital in Wilmington, Delaware, after suffering a brain aneurysm.

The likable lefty was one of the most popular players on the ill-fated '64 squad. He was nicknamed "Style" for his evident indifference to "threads," as Johnny Callison called clothes back in the day.

Sartorial sensitivities aside, "Style" was a '64 All-Star and vital cog in his team's success. He finished 23rd in MVP Award voting in '64. His 2.20 ERA placed him third in the NL that season behind a tandem of Dodger future Hall of Famers named Koufax (1.74) and Drysdale (2.18). In hits per nine innings pitched, IP, walks, and shutouts (4), Short ranked among the NL's top three hurlers. Ironically, his .654

won-lost percentage landed him in seventh position in the NL, directly behind his Phillies portside predecessor, Curt Simmons.

Shorty's teammates at the 1989 reunion were hushed and humbled by his plight. Former Short stablemate Art Mahaffey spent months prior to the get-together organizing a benefit golf tournament for Short. The tournament was a big success. It took place the Monday before the reunion and netted $46,000 to help defray Short's medical expenses. During the reunion weekend, the '64 Phillies autographed 4,826 throwback hats. The batch of hats, priced at $10 per hat, sold out at Veterans Stadium with all proceeds going to Chris and his wife, Pat.

JOHN CALLISON: "Style and I basically came up and matured together as Phils. I had spent a couple of years with the White Sox before coming to Philly in 1960, but I was only 19 when I was in Chicago. I only played about 50 games there with barely 100 at-bats. When I got to Philly, I was green. Chris Short had come up briefly with the Phils in 1959, but I'm sure he hadn't even pitched 15 innings. So basically, we were rookies in 1960. It wasn't an easy start for either of us. The Phils finished in last place that season. Then things got really awful the next year!"

Callison was referring to the Phillies' 1961 "23 skidoo." The hapless Phils lost 23 games in a row in 1961 en route to a 47–107 worst-in-baseball last-place finish.

CALLISON: "They were depressing, forgettable days. Neither Style or I was burning up the league. I finally got a starting berth in '61, but I had a really disappointing season. My average was .266, and I hit fewer than 10 homers. Style was unhappy with his performance, too. [Short was 6–9 and 6–12 respectively in '60 and '61 with a 5.94 ERA in '61.] I remember some conversations with Style when we were both down and couldn't see our way up. Young guys like us started doubting ourselves, wondering if we belonged in baseball at this level. You can't give enough credit to our manager, Gene Mauch, for guiding us through those personal struggles. He fought hard to prevent Short and me and some others from getting down on ourselves. I thank Mauch for helping Shorty and me come into our own after some bleak years early on."

Manager Gene Mauch was a tough, often surly guy who didn't mince words and did *not* have a love affair with the Philly media. But he was a steadfast, devoted cheerleader for both Short and Callison. Mauch never lost faith in them—at least not that he let on.

JACK BALDSCHUN, Phillies 1960s relief pitcher: "Style always had good stuff, amazing stuff. The Dodgers were always saying Chris Short's stuff was better than any other lefty's in the league–excluding Sandy Koufax, of course. Coming from Sandy Koufax's team, that was high praise. Shorty put up great numbers once he gained confidence. I believe he had his breakout or turnaround year somewhere about '62—the same year our team made its turnaround. [Baldschun was correct. The '62 Phils went 81–80, posting, though barely, their first better-than-.500 season since 1953. Short was 11–9 that year, which was his first winning record in MLB]. Short could handle righties, lefties. It didn't matter. He got them all out. He was one of the rare pitchers who basically had no weaknesses in his game."

Short's 1964 numbers back up Baldschun's words. In '64, Short held left-handed hitters to a .217 average and righties to a .218 average. In away games, he held batters to a .217 average; in home games, opponents batted .218.

Dennis Bennett, another tough Phillies lefty in the sixties, spins a funny story about Shorty.

DENNIS BENNETT, Phillies 1960s left-handed pitcher: "Hey, first of all, the Dodgers thought I was a tough lefty, too. Walter Alston, the Dodgers manager, always said I gave his team fits. Alston gave me quite an honor in '64. My best season was '63 when I went 9–5 with a 2.64 ERA. The Dodgers won the '63 pennant, so Alston managed the NL squad in the '64 All-Star Game. Alston called me personally and asked me to pitch batting practice for the NL before the game. I was thrilled.

"As for Style, he had a squeaky-clean image with the press. But he could be a funny guy with an unusual sense of humor when he was out with the boys. Our team was sworn to secrecy for years about this story, but I think it's safe to tell all these years later.

"We had to travel to Eugene [Oregon] for an exhibition game against our Single A farm club right in the midst of the '64 pennant race. [Pitcher] Ed Roebuck, [catcher] Clay Dalrymple, and Style were having some kind of problem at a Chinese restaurant. I was an eye-witness! I was eating dinner across the street with my parents, and I watched the whole thing at the Chinese place play out. All of a sudden, there was some kind of big disturbance—about what, I'm not really sure. Shorty and the other guys never really did come clean. But anyway, Roebuck wound up breaking a plate-glass window in the fracas. After that, he started running away down the street with this terrified look on his face. Here's the thing—Eddie could *not* run. Watching him run was funny enough. But then he turned his ankle and fell, which I'm sure was painful. But I have to admit, it was also funny to watch in a Keystone cop kind of way.

"The Phils and the press kept the episode under wraps. The Phils paid for the window. But it didn't turn out too funny for us because the bad ankle affected Ed's pitching. He never pitched as effectively again after that. Eddie told me later that, besides the ankle problem, his roommate, Dallas Green, spent that night pulling slivers of glass out of his shoulders. As I said, Style was at the scene, but, like usual, he just kind of slipped out of the picture unscathed. But I watched him walking up the street laughing his butt off at the whole comedy. That was typical Chris Short. Nothing bothered him anytime, anywhere—but especially on the mound."

Sadly, Style never regained consciousness after slipping into a coma in October 1988. On August 1, 1991, he succumbed and died. He was survived by his wife, Pat, and three sons, Rhawn, Nicky, and Eric.

Lefty

Despite the feats of every member of the Phils' elite quartet of portsiders, the name "Lefty" is the exclusive domain of the most illustrious of the group, Steve Carlton. Carlton arrived in Philadelphia via the trade route. The Cards swapped him for Phillie Rick Wise, a fan-favorite 25-year-old pitcher coming off a 17–14, 2.88 All-Star campaign.

JOHN VUKOVICH, Phillies third baseman and coach: "Rick Wise had what I'll always say is the best game I ever saw a major league pitcher have, bar none. He no-hit the Reds. Well, that's a feat in itself because he did it when they had Rose, Bench, Concepcion, Foster, and Lee May in the lineup. But Wise also hit two home runs that same night! I caught the last out of the game, a scorcher off the bat of Pete Rose. I'd have killed myself if I'd have missed that one and cost Wise his no-hitter."

But Steve Carlton was also a known, respected, and envied commodity in baseball. As a 22-year-old, he made his first World Series appearance. Although he lost his only Series start in '67, Lefty's 2.98 ERA that season equaled that of three-game '67 World Series winner and Series MVP Bob Gibson.

The Cardinals plummeted to fourth place by 1969. Their star was falling, but Carlton's star was on the rise. His ERA that year was 2.17. Teammate Bob Gibson, the most dominant pitcher in the NL, posted a 2.18 ERA. By 1971, Lefty had taken the legendary 35-year-old Gibson's role as the ace of the staff, leading the team with a 20–9 record.

The following year, Lefty found himself in Philadelphia poised for one of the most prodigious seasons in baseball history. In 1972, Lefty started 41 games, completed 30, and hurled eight shutouts. He won 27, struck out 310, and walked only 87 in 346⅓ innings. His ERA was 1.97 and his WHIP (walks plus hits over innings pitched) was 0.993. His K/BB ratio was 3.56. He led the NL in every one of those categories and was the consensus choice for the Cy Young Award.

Not apparent in those glowing stats, however, is his most stunning achievement. He earned those 27 wins pitching for a terrible albeit promising young team that won only 59 games. That means Carlton accounted for 45.8 percent of his team's victories—a post-1901 major league record. Lefty is one of only 10 pitchers since 1901 who accounted for more than 40 percent of his team's total wins for a season, and he's the only one to do so since 1922 when Eddie Rommel chipped in 27 of the Philadelphia A's 65 wins.

Pitcher Steve Carlton serves up a three-hit shutout against the Pirates in Pittsburgh on August 9, 1972. Carlton won his 13th consecutive game, a Phillies club record, by beating the Pirates 2–0. *(AP Photo/GRG)*

MAJE McDONNELL, Mr. Phillie for six decades: "I caught the tail end of Rommel's career. He was a huge favorite in this town. I saw him when I was a kid and Rommel was at the end of his career. He was still effective but a lesser light on those Hall of Fame–filled 1929–31 A's teams. Anyone would be a lesser light on a team with Lefty Grove on it! Lefty Grove and Lefty Carlton—they were the two greatest lefties this town ever saw, and maybe that *any* town ever saw."

"Video Dan" Stephenson, the Phils' longtime videographer, spent a lot of time talking with Lefty Carlton over the years.

VIDEO DAN STEPHENSON: "Lefty had his own training routine. He brought Gus Hoefling here to Philly with him. Gus became the Phils' strength and fitness coach. The team thought so much of Gus, they awarded him a World Series ring in 1980.

"Lefty was an unusual guy, one of the most interesting guys who ever played here. He had his own ideas on just about everything. He had his own specific conditioning program. He never missed it. He went through it daily with Gus. Doing something kind of rogue like that in those days was sort of frowned upon. Everyone else in baseball would obediently do whatever the club made them do for fitness—and the ball clubs didn't know much, if anything, about fitness. Lefty was miles out ahead of them.

"When Lefty was in the midst of that monster year in '72, the press was kind of fascinated by his conditioning program. They thought it was a little weird, but since Lefty was dominating baseball, nobody spoke negatively about it. The following year, some people forget Lefty had a bad year. He lost 20 [and won only 13]. The press started making snickering remarks about Lefty's conditioning program, which they called his 'kung fu stuff.' Lefty was touchy about his routine. He didn't appreciate the remarks or what he perceived as the press turning on him.

"Lefty was dead serious about winning—dead serious every time he went to the mound. He got fed up with the press and laid down the rule: 'I'm not talking to the press. Never. No matter what the circumstances.'"

"He stuck to that rule his entire career, even when *Sports Illustrated* came here to do a special story on him when he was about to break the all-time strikeout record. Lefty refused to grant them an interview. He told them, 'Policy is policy.' I can still hear him saying it!"

JOHN VUKOVICH: "Lefty had what I'd call the most amazing 'unintentional' sense of humor I've ever seen. I don't know what else to call it, but here's what I mean.

"I was traded in '72 to Milwaukee. Don Money [3B], Billy Champion [pitcher], and I were dealt away for Ken Brett, Jim Lonborg, Ken Sanders, and Earl Stephenson. I came back to Philly from 1976–81. That whole time, Lefty was the most dominant pitcher in baseball. Anyway, after I came back, Joe Hoerner, who pitched with Lefty on those sixties teams in St. Louis, was traded to Philly. When we all welcomed Hoerner into the fold, I remember Hoerner begging Lefty: 'Lefty, now that we're back as teammates, you gotta show me how to throw that killer slider of yours.' Lefty promised he would. A few weeks later, I asked Hoerner how he was making out with the slider Lefty was teaching him. Hoerner laughed, 'Lefty's not what you'd call a gifted teacher. I kept asking him how to throw the slider and all he'd tell me was: "Simple. Just grip the ball like this and throw the hell out of it." Well, I tried it. It worked for Lefty, but it sure as hell didn't work for me!'"

Tim McCarver, another Cardinals transplant, became Lefty's designated catcher.

TIM McCARVER: "I never saw anyone concentrate on the mound like Lefty and Bob Gibson. I had the honor of catching both those guys. Catching Lefty was like having a catch in the backyard. He knew exactly where he wanted to put every pitch. I'd toss the ball back to him, and he'd pitch it in to that spot. To him, it was like the batter wasn't even there."

Darren Daulton, fan favorite and rookie teammate of Carlton in 1983, was amazed at how unpretentious Lefty was.

DARREN DAULTON: "I came up to the Phils for the first time in '83. That's when I first met Lefty. The guy was so down to earth I was shocked. He didn't have a trace of big-timer attitude. But he absolutely refused to talk to reporters. He'd have fit right in with our '93 team! We weren't fond of talking with the press, either."

VIDEO DAN: "Part of Gus' conditioning program called for Lefty to push his hand down through a rice-filled barrel until he touched the bottom. Sound easy? That's what Joe Morgan thought. When Joe played here in '83, he asked Lefty what the rice barrel was for. Lefty explained it to him, and Joe tried to sink his hand into it. Joe didn't get much farther than the palm of his hand, and Joe was a compact guy who prided himself on his strength. You should have seen Joe's face when Lefty said, 'Watch this,' reached in and, in about two seconds, was shoulder deep in the rice barrel. Joe thought there was a trick. There wasn't. That's just how strong Lefty was.

"And let me tell you how competitive Carlton was. One day, I was sitting in the video room with GG [Greg Gross]. Suddenly we heard this grunting and yelling out in the tunnels in the old Vet. It was Gus taking Lefty through his workout. Lefty had already won his 20th game that year. We had clinched. Most guys would be winding down, chilling, taking it easy 'til playoff time. Not Lefty. As GG put it, 'Listen to that. Lefty's got a couple more starts. But he's going to punish himself up to the bitter end whether the game counts or not! He can't stand losing.'

"Lefty left Philly with a smile. He always had supreme confidence. He believed firmly he'd pitch 'til he was 50. For a long while, it looked like he would. His delivery always seemed fluid and effortless. But looks are deceiving. Before he left, a doctor checked him out and asked him how long his arm had been hurting. Lefty told him, 'About four years.' Four years. Amazing! He had won 15 games with a 3.11 ERA a few years earlier, and he did it with a sore arm. He just never told anyone. His arm probably even pained him the year he won his fourth Cy Young Award.

"One incident I'll never forget involved Lefty and another all-time great, Johnny Bench. Bench owned Carlton. That happens in baseball from time to time. It's unexplainable, but it exists. Tommy Hutton owned Tom Seaver. He batted .320 against him, far above his .248 lifetime average. Bench hit three home runs in a game *twice* against Carlton [Bench had one other three-homer against the Padres' Randy Jones]. Anyway, it was fairly early in the season [May 4, 1983], and the Reds were in town. Bench was looking for his 2,000[th] career hit. Lefty was on the mound. He got ahead of Bench 0–2 and then threw him about eight straight wicked sliders. Bench fought every one of them off. I'm sure if you asked Bench, he'd have no idea how he managed to make contact on some of them. Then on about the 10th pitch of the at-bat, Bench ripped a double to left. When Bench was standing on second, Lefty straddled the rubber and then turned completely around to face Bench on second. Lefty took his hat off and bowed. I thought, *What a moment I just witnessed! Two giants of the game battling each other tooth and nail, and then one paying homage to the other for besting him.* Here's the kicker. I've mentioned that incident several times to Lefty—he doesn't remember it! That's because his concentration was so intense that all he ever thought of was getting the next guy out. By the time Lefty turned around to face the next batter, that moment was erased from his memory. The only thing he was focused on was his next pitch."

Cole

After our book, *More Than Beards, Bellies and Biceps*, was released in 2003, co-author Tom Burgoyne and I had the honor of participating in the Hall of Fame Game's weekend program in Cooperstown. The game pitted the Phillies against the Tampa Bay Rays. Since the Phillies were in town, the organizers figured correctly that Cooperstown would be crawling with members of the Phillies Nation. So Tom and I were invited as guest speakers for the Hall of Fame's "Dugout Talk" that year. It was an honor, but a no-brainer for the organizers. Anybody who knows anything about Phillies fans knows they relish every opportunity to hear tales about their city's most cherished team, the '93 Phils.

The 2003 Hall of Fame Game program was awesome for fans. There were some interesting talks as well as a blockbuster interview with Gary Carter who was being inducted into the Hall later that summer. But the best part for fans was getting to hobnob with former baseball greats. Any time Cooperstown hosts a major league powwow of any kind—particularly one of this magnitude—a bevy of baseball's retirees roll into town. Fans spend a few days populating a dreamscape where former stars actually walk among us, though often on wobbly and weary legs. For a few magic days, fans and stars stitch together, side by side, into Cooperstown's Disney-esque fabric. You never know whom you might bump into. What's more, as time marches on, ex-stars become more approachable and more likely to engage in lengthy, candid discussions.

Too bad the Hall did away with those games. A half-decade after the 2003 tilt, the annual contest was abandoned.

The inter-league series had a long run. It lasted from 1940 to 2008. A beautiful stadium, Doubleday Field, was erected for the games. It was sited in Elihu Phinney's cow pasture—the location where tradition places the first baseball game ever played. The Doubleday name was a nostalgic tip of the hat to baseball's creator, Abner Doubleday. Unfortunately, as is typical of most creation myths, baseball's version—while idyllic and soulfully satisfying—is, alas, errant. Just as Roman tales relate how Romulus founded the city after being suckled and raised by a she-wolf, or just as American schoolchildren recite the poem of Paul Revere and his swashbuckling ride to warn every Middlesex village and farm that the British were coming, the story of how baseball was invented fails vetting. Romulus wasn't raised by a she-wolf. Paul Revere was arrested by the British before reaching his destination. Obviously, the British were already *in* Concord. And baseball's founding yarn—that Abner Doubleday invented baseball—is also a tall tale that doesn't stand up to the scrutiny of serious scholarship.

As baseball's founding myth would have us believe, Abner invented baseball in 1839 when he gathered the town folks together in Phinney's cow pasture to unveil his new game. Everybody tossed the old cowhide around. Fathers bonded with sons. Dogs barked. Fine-skirted ladies cheered. Yes, that's the whimsical kind of debut our pastoral (and for that very reason, former) national pastime craves. But Abner, as research has shown, wasn't even *in* Cooperstown in 1839. He was a cadet at West Point. Before dismissing ol' Abner Doubleday, however, I have to point out that he stakes another historical claim that is not factitious.

Legitimate historians finger Abner Doubleday, at least at present, as the one who fired the first shot of the Civil War at Fort Sumter.

The creation myth notwithstanding, no facts about baseball's birth can diminish the beauty of the lovely little Victorian gem that is Cooperstown, nor of the spectacular stage it sets for the patrimony of our national pastime. Cooperstown simply *feels* like the place where baseball was birthed. And if it was not, it should have been—just as Tarrytown, some 100 miles south of Cooperstown, *feels* like there's truly a headless horseman thundering through the midnight mist at harvest time. Sometimes it's more fun to allow truthiness to trump truth.

Suffice it to say, Doubleday Field itself is a beautiful structure that wistfully evokes long-ago sunny days when clean air wafted summer scents over wide-open fields where kids in knickers played ball on makeshift diamonds. A wooden grandstand was built in 1924 and was replaced in 1939 when Franklin D. Roosevelt's Work Progress Administration erected a steel and concrete grandstand.

As for the annual Hall of Fame Game itself, the affair started off as an old-timers' contest. It wasn't until 1940 that it morphed into an interleague exhibition—a tradition that lasted until 2008.

What killed the tradition? In the modern era with its more demanding 162-game schedule, the ballplayers became increasingly unwilling participants. They preferred time off to logging another workday. Management felt the same way. With skyrocketing salaries upping the investment in each player, owners feared unnecessary, increased exposure to accidents and injuries.

Scheduling teams became increasingly problematic. Thirty teams routinely crisscrossed the country playing 162 single games since the doubleheader went the way of the nickel candy bar, the double-feature, and grace in political campaigns. An expanded postseason schedule ramped up the pressure to cram the entirety of the regular season into the allotted time. All wiggle room is gone.

But it was regular season interleague play that dealt the deathblow. The attraction of seeing "the other league" play—a treat fans formerly got to savor only in the All-Star Game and World Series—was removed. So little by little, the luster of the traditional Hall of Fame Game faded away like the smell of cigar smoke at the old ballyard.

Of course, when I spoke at the Hall of Fame Game festivities in 2003, I couldn't have known that by 2008, the game itself would be history. I had an inkling, an educated notion, that its days were numbered. But baseball pundits have no shortage of hunches and notions, such as the days of the designated hitter are numbered (I'm looking at you, American League), or the days of *not* having a designated hitter are numbered (I'm looking at you, National League).

More relevantly, however, on that June day in 2003, I had no notion or premonition that in 2008, the very same year the Annual NL-AL Doubleday Field Exhibition Game would become history, these very same combatants—the Phillies and the Rays—would battle for a world championship. Nor did I have a premonition that one of the 2003 game's stars, in fact, the game's biggest star—a kid I met on that Hall of Fame Game weekend—would be the MVP of that 2008 World Series.

The 2008 World Series MVP needs no introduction. As every Philadelphia Phillies fan knows, he is Colbert (pronounced like Nate Colbert, not Stephen Colbert) Michael Hamels. Cole was born on December 27, 1983, in San Diego. He was drafted in the first round of the 2002 Amateur Draft, the 217th selection overall. Hamels had a spectacular minor league career prior to his ballyhooed arrival in Philadelphia in 2006 where he made his major league debut on May 12, 2006. That day, he further fueled the high expectations that the Phillies organization and its fans had for him when he tossed a five-inning, one-hit, no-run gem in a game the Phillies eventually won 8–4 over Cincinnati.

But when I met Cole Hamels at the Hall of Fame Game, he was a 20-year old rookie that the Phils had called up from wa-a-a-y down in the minors. That's another aspect of the old Annual Hall of Fame clash at Doubleday Field—regulars, as I mentioned, didn't want to play. And by 2003, they usually *didn't* or, if they did, they made a cameo appearance.

So in its later years, to a great extent the Hall of Fame Game devolved into a contest between the two opponents' top farm prospects.

Cole Hamels was pressed into service for the 2003 game after his first couple of months as a professional baseball player. At the time of the 2003 game, Hamels was assigned to the Phils' Class A Lakewood (New Jersey) Blue Claws club. He had also played for the Clearwater Single A club that year.

Playing for the parent club at age 20 didn't overwhelm Cole Hamels—far from it. I saw the game. Like many dyed-in-the-wool Phillies fans, I didn't need to say, "Who *is* this guy?" Hamels was already a prized commodity in a Phillies organization that projected big things from him. And big things are what Hamels delivered in his first big-league situation. Hamels stole the show.

A pair of young hopefuls looked good that day. One was Frank Brooks, who got the win. Unfortunately, that game was practically his last hurrah. Brooks was pitching for the Reading Phils when he was whisked off to Cooperstown for the Hall of Fame Game. Not long afterward, he was shuffled over to Pittsburgh in exchange for 34-year-old Mike Williams and cash. Brooks pitched a total of 17.2 major league innings during the next two seasons before calling it quits. Williams suffered through an 0–4, 5.96 ERA 2003 season for the Phils. He hung up his spikes at season's end.

There is more to the Mike Williams story—it's unusual. Mike had been a 2002 All-Star for the Bucs. He was their lone representative on the 2003 All-Star squad. Strangely, it's not that no other Pirates were worthy. That year, Jason Kendall, one of the era's better catchers batted a lofty .325 in 587 at-bats. A 35-year-old Reggie Sanders socked 31 home runs with 87 RBIs and a .285 batting average. Neither was chosen for the squad. Only Mike Williams—with his 1–3, 6.27 line at game time—made the field.

In the 2003 Hall of Fame Game, Cole Hamels struck out nine in five innings of work. His hurling allowed the Phils to overcome an early deficit thanks to homers by Pat Burrell and Nick Punto.

I had a chance to meet Cole after his impressive debut.

COLE HAMELS: "I certainly can't take too much away from one performance. I felt good. I felt comfortable out there, but I know I have a lot more to show before I earn a spot on this staff. It's a great staff. Kevin Millwood just threw a no-hitter. [Millwood no-hit the Giants less than two months before, on April 27, 2003.] Vicente Padilla was an All-Star last year, and he's pitching great again this year. Randy Wolf is a talented pitcher, and so is Brett Myers. They're all pretty young, too. [At that point, Millwood, at 28, was the oldest of the quartet. Myers, at 22, was the youngest.] It's going to be tough breaking in. But yes, I am happy about making a good showing today, although I wasn't the only one striking people out. [There were 25 whiffs in the game, a Hall of Fame Game record]."

At that point in his career, Cole Hamels was only a few years removed from being a freshman and sophomore phenom at Rancho Bernardo High School in San Diego County, California. His fastball at the time was clocked in the low- to mid-90s. It was surprising that he escaped the notice of the San Diego Padres.

HAMELS: "I broke my arm in my sophomore year at Rancho Bernardo. After that, I wasn't nearly as hot a commodity. The Padres showed some interest, but I was happy when the Phils drafted me in the first round. That was an honor."

When Cole said he hurt his arm in high school, he was understating. He broke it stunningly and frighteningly. The break occurred in a summer-league game in 2000 after his sophomore year at Rancho Bernardo. His humerus—the bone between the shoulder and elbow—simply snapped and shattered as he was releasing the ball.

HAMELS: "Such pain! I was writhing on the ground. I couldn't see anything. I was in such pain. They tell me the pitch flew over the backstop."

Injuries delayed Cole's taking the fast track to superstardom. In his first three years in pro ball, he tossed only 152 innings—all in the minors. From the status of red-hot phenom, his stock among the smart baseball guys plummeted. At one point, *Baseball Prospectus* described him as "Fabergé eggs, china dolls, and ice sculptures."

In 2005, Cole's march to the bigs was further derailed when he fractured his pitching hand, thanks to the most puzzling, regrettable, and uncharacteristic incident of his life—a much-publicized bar fight in Clearwater at a place called Razzel's Lounge.

Cole Hamels has come a long way since the incident. A scant three years later, he won the MVP in both the NLCS and the World Series. He pitched with aplomb, finesse, and savvy beyond his years—enough to impress the old pitching master himself, the Yoda of the art of hurling, Jamie Moyer.

I've had the pleasure of following Jamie's career for years in our local paper, *The North Penn Reporter* [renamed *The Reporter*]. Jamie attended nearby Souderton Area High School and practically owned the sports page for the entirety of his high school career. After the 2008 victory, I asked Jamie for his opinion of the Phillies' bright young pitching star.

JAMIE MOYER: "The sky's the limit for Cole. I'm amazed by the guy's mound maturity. He already pitches in a way that veteran pitchers have to evolve into. In fact, most don't or can't. It's a natural style for Cole. When fastballers lose a little off their fastball, they have to start fine-tuning their pitches. They need to rely on keeping hitters off-balance and keep them guessing instead of just blowing them away with good stuff. Most guys are forced into doing that. Cole does it because that's the way he pitches. He has the great stuff of a young pitcher, but he adds the maturity and savvy of a crafty veteran. I *never* had that great fastball Cole has. And his changeup is one of the best I've ever seen. He has the same release point for all his pitches, so batters can't tell what's coming. Everything that comes out of his hand looks the same. It comes from the same spot but at different speeds, and it goes to different spots: inside, outside, down, up. I catch with Cole on a regular basis, and I'm always amazed at the movement on his ball even when we have a catch."

Cole Hamels has come a long way from his early career when injuries slowed down his advancement. He's come a long way off the field, as well.

Cole is one of Philly's top citizens. Make that Cole and his wife, Heidi (née Strobel), have become one of Philly's finest couples

Heidi was a contestant on *Survivor* in the show's sixth season. She was a viewer favorite and parlayed her fame into a succession of celebrity appearances. One of them led her to Bright House Field in 2004 where Cole Hamels was pitching. The two met, and the rest is history.

Cole Hamels' young career is impressive—big-time impressive. Besides his NLCS and World Series' MVP awards, Cole is a three-time All-Star who has won 10 or more games for six straight seasons. Twice his won-lost percentages topped .700. And twice his yearly strikeout total has exceeded 200.

The sky was the limit for Cole Hamels as the 20-year-old who stole the show in Cooperstown. For 28-year-old Cole Hamels, the sky is still the limit—it's just a bigger sky.

chapter 7

Phanatics

Who holds the legitimate claim to being Philly's finest, most phamous immigrant? The answer's a piece of cake! No, a piece of cake is not the answer. I mean the answer is easy, clear. Like the Highlander, there can be only one. This particular one is big and green and recognized worldwide. And despite being perpetually speechless, this idol and icon never ever loses phaith in Philly's Phillies.

If you're still stumped, you've been asleep for the past 33 years or so. And that would be impossible, at least in the City of Brotherly Love. Sure, New York claims to be the city that never sleeps. But sleepless in the Big Apple owes to days of maddening traffic, nonstop hostility, push-and-shove perambulation, and working three jobs a day just to pay the rent followed by sleepless nights worrying about paying the astronomical, absurd stipends required to live in a tiny walk-up that would make your mother cry if she ever risked visiting (unless of course discouraging parental visits is the reason you moved there in the first place).

Phweww! Philly has become a town that doesn't sleep, too–but for far more civilized reasons. We have superb theaters, amazing restaurants, and a world-class art scene. Above all, Philly is simply crazy about its sports teams. And aside from the year 2012, it's hard to sleep through the streak of domination that the Phils rode from 2007–11, although in fairness and thankfulness to the Mets, we do have to tip our hats for their accommodating habit of folding during pennant races and paving the way for the Phils to grab the flag. The Metropolitans of NYC have ceded division honors to the Phillies with the same easy-come-easy-go abandon used by the Big Apple's mayor as he shells out dollars to get elected.

The Phillie Phanatic during a game against the Florida Marlins on Friday, August 7, 2009, in Philadelphia. *(AP Photo/Matt Slocum)*

But let's return to the question of Philadelphia's top immigrant. As any real Philadelphian will tell you, the answer is the Phillie Phanatic. That's a gimme in Philly, although it wasn't the answer until 1978 when he arrived in the Quaker City. Before then, any schoolkid who could correctly spell "Philadelphia" knew that Ben Franklin was Philly's most famous immigrant. Residents of the City of Brotherly Love knew that Ben Franklin came to Philadelphia from Boston—the reverse of the journey, albeit more circuitous, that the history-bucking Curt Schilling took. In choosing cheesesteaks over beans, Ben demonstrated the kind of discriminating wisdom that endeared him forever to his adopted city. We should be thankful that Ben set out for Philly before Boston's Big Dig commenced. Otherwise, Ben might never have reached the banks of the Delaware in time to found our town's first hospital, library, and fire insurance company.

Sadly, Ben's reign as Philly's most famous immigrant indeed came to an end, as must the reign of all good things, with the arrival in Philadelphia of a strange-looking, stranger-acting green creature from the Galápagos Islands.

Who is the Phanatic? His official bio goes something like this:

The Phillie Phanatic is a strange creature that stowed away on a boat out of the Galápagos Islands in 1978 and made port in Philadelphia. By pure serendipity, he wandered into Veteran's Stadium. He stowed away and hid somewhere in the bowels (appropriate choice of words) of the now-demolished structure. By and by, he emerged from the shadows, like a latter-day Phantom of the Vet, but without the mask or the great singing voice yet with the same eye for beautiful women. When he set foot on the great faux-grass greenery that was the Vet carpet, he was smitten. The hulking creature was fascinated by a group of guys in red pinstripes, many of whom sported bizarre moustaches. Looking at photos of that comically coifed era, one could dispute who looked more strange, the Phanatic or the players in the seventies.

As a Galápagos native who grew up surrounded by species found nowhere else, this recent immigrant was not shocked by this peculiar breed of scraggly, long-haired, mustachioed *homo sapiens*. Nor was he shocked by the vividly green-yet-unnatural-and-sickly-looking phony grass that was not actually growing all around. Perhaps he dismissed the repugnant Astroturf as a cruel mistake of natural selection.

For whatever reason, Philly's huge green immigrant was hooked on Philly and the circular stadium he had stumbled upon. He fell in love with the guys in the red pinstripes and the game of baseball.

Pitch

BILL GILES: "I don't know. Why don't we use that intern, Raymond? He's cocky. He could do it."

Bill Giles, the former Phillies president and chairman of the board, was hit off-guard as he stammered a hipshot response at a meeting with the Phillies staff. Giles had just proposed a bold new idea intended to draw people into the Phillies' relatively new yet already older-than-its-years home, Veterans Stadium.

BILL GILES: "I had just been out to San Diego. I was fascinated by the Chicken Man. The guy electrified the stadium. I couldn't help envisioning something like that for the Philly fans. I was convinced they'd eat it up. But at the time, mascots for professional teams were unheard of. So when I proposed the idea to the Phils, well, let's just say it wasn't an easy sell. Besides, I myself had just kind of a vague notion about how it would work. When I first proposed it, I admit I hadn't worked through many specifics."

What would the mascot look like? What would he do? What would his name be? Who would design him? Who would you put inside the costume?

The Phils' brass had spent the early part of the seventies working through the details of building a good baseball team—a skill that Phillies front offices had never mastered during their 95 years of existence. By 1978, the Phils finally had matters between the stripes moving in the right direction. In Bill Giles' reckoning, they finally had the luxury of diverting some attention from the field to more whimsical affairs, such as being the first franchise in MLB to contract a mascot.

Let's revisit where the Phils stood in 1977 in terms of fielding a contending team. They had slinked out of the sixties with an abysmal 63–99 (.389, 37 GB) record, which was not quite "good" enough to land them in the cellar. The admission of the Montreal Expos into the NL in 1969 saved them that embarrassment for two years. But in 1971, the Phils reclaimed the cellar, and they occupied it for the next three years. However, change was coming. In 1974, Philadelphia zoomed up to third place, missing the .500 mark by only two games. In 1975, they burst through the .500 barrier for the first time since 1967 and finished in second place. Behind a cast of mostly home-grown young stars such as Mike Schmidt, Larry Bowa, Greg Luzinski, and Bob Boone, the Phils morphed not only into legitimate contenders but frontrunners. They finished first in the NL East Division in 1976 and '77.

At that point, Bill Giles reassessed the business of baseball and perhaps reinvented pieces of it.

BILL GILES: "Society was changing. Baseball had to change, as well, or it would die. That change entailed remaking the image of the game and creating appeal for newer generations. Insiders had to rethink and modernize baseball as it was currently presented to the public. They had to adopt the notion that baseball, when you get down to it, is simply a form of entertainment that competes with all other forms of entertainment for the entertainment dollar. That's why the mascot thing took hold of me. I knew we had to start looking for attractions beyond the draw of what happened on the field itself. We had to reach out and appeal to new, young generations that thrived on fast-paced, nontraditional entertainment.

"The younger generations weren't playing baseball like they used to. Baseball required too much space, too much equipment, and too much time for modern kids. There isn't space for fields in inner cities like there had been in previous generations. Kids were playing basketball almost to the exclusion of baseball because basketball was faster-paced and all you need to play is a basketball and a hoop. Baseball needed to accept that shift and start to consciously appeal to the youth. A mascot seemed to fall in line with that."

But how to roll that idea out—how to start from a vague concept, sell it to peers who think you've lost your mind, and once sold, how to proceed—well, all that wasn't so simple.

BILL GILES: "I hired an outfit in New York to come up with a design for the costume. They had worked with Jim Henson creating the Sesame Street characters. In an initial mockup, they came up with something I though was pretty good. Actually, it was pretty much the Phanatic that you see right now. That's what I took to the management meeting where I pitched the idea. I took their drawings and mockups. I guess I was a little over the top about the look and the design and a little light on details.

"But the Phils did like the look and the idea. The problem was when they hit me with who exactly I had in mind to put inside the costume, I was unprepared. I just blurted out, 'How about that Raymond kid.'"

Everybody Loves Raymond

Dave Raymond, the first human to don the Phillie Phanatic costume, smiles when he recalls the day the Phillies called and offered him a job— or a hazy facsimile of a job.

DAVE RAYMOND: "I thought my fraternity brothers were punking me, just pulling a prank of some kind. I came back to the fraternity house during my final semester at the University of Delaware, and I had a message that read, 'Dave, call the Phillies about a job.'

"I had worked for the Phils as an intern a couple of summers. I helped Frank Sullivan, the Phillies promotions director at the time. I worked on a bunch of different things, like the '76 All-Star Game festivities. The game was played at the Vet that year. The last thing I was expecting was a job offer, though. I had no idea what job it could have been for.

"So thinking it was just a fraternity prank, I played along. I called Frank back and soon realized the call was legit in one sense but not quite legit or conventional in another. The first thing I heard when Frank answered was Chrissy Long yelling in the background, 'Dave! Just say no! Say no!' I had no idea why she was screaming until Frank explained that the Phillies were indeed offering me a job. Okay, sounded good so far. Then he explained the nature of the job. It's more like he *tried* to explain the nature of the job. When he did, I realized Chrissie had every right to be screaming.

"Frank said the Phils—and Mr. Giles in particular—wanted me to be their new mascot. They wanted me to crawl inside a big Sesame Street character-type suit and then—well, the job description got fuzzy from there on.

"Mascot? I'm thinking, *This is really gonna go down well with my parents! Four years of college to wear a clown suit.* Parents are full of surprises, though. My parents were all for it. They were old school. They figured when an employer—even a past employer—asks you to do something, you do it. No questions asked. So I accepted the offer, and I asked only one short, easy question, 'What do I actually have to *do?*' I asked Frank and everyone else I talked to. I got the same response from everybody. They laughed. I figured they were laughing like, 'What a *stupid* question! Why do you even have to ask? Isn't it obvious?' I realized a short time later their laugh was more like, 'How the hell would I know?'

"You want to know the most amazing thing? The Phils sent me a drawing of the costume. I had this vague visual image, but I never actually saw the real-deal costume until the night I put it on and headed into the crowd as the Phillie Phanatic!"

That night was April 25, 1978. And as you can readily assume, the Phils and their new mascot had every move carefully orchestrated. We're talking here about the slick, multi-billion-dollar baseball industry. The introduction of the Phillie Phanatic was undoubtedly calibrated with precision—Beta tested, shown to countless focus groups, tweaked by voluminous feedback. Nothing was left to chance. Right, Dave?

DAVE RAYMOND: "We had not a clue what we were going to do that first night. We had no idea how the fans were going to react. After all, these were Philly fans. We all know the Santa Claus–snowball story."

Dave's got a point. Philly fans are portrayed (inaccurately I believe) as the kind of heartless cynics who watch *It's a Wonderful Life* and root for

Mr. Potter or who leave *Old Yeller* vindicated, convinced that Old Yeller had it coming.

DAVE RAYMOND: "My only instructions came from Bill Giles who told me, 'Just kind of interact with the fans and see what happens.' That was pretty much it. Sort of open ended, wouldn't you say? Before the game I went down on the field. Tony Taylor was there, muttering something in Spanish about 'cojones.' I can't help you with that one. I don't speak Spanish. I hung around Ted Sizemore, Bake McBride, Garry Maddox, and a bunch of other players. They had no idea what I was or what I was doing. I didn't either. That made us even.

"In the third inning, I made my debut with the fans. I just kind of waded into the crowd behind the plate in the 200-level and flamed and flailed around, trying to get some sort of reaction that would make for an interesting obituary. I was amazed. These were really good times for the Phils. There was an electric buzz around the park. The Phils finished first the previous two years. So I agree with Mr. Giles; the time was right. The fans viewed this bizarre mascot as something special—an added attraction at the park, rather that a diversion to keep the fans' eyes off a bad team on the field. For whatever reason, the fans were great. They were into everything I did. They made it easy.

"I strolled down to the old picnic area. Remember that at the Vet? I started messing with the people there who were having a picnic. They were mostly there to party anyway. So I partied. I hopped from table to table. They thought it was great. I became part of their fun.

"What a dynamite debut! The Phils won 7–0. Jim Kaat pitched a complete-game shutout over the Cubs. I felt like the team's good luck charm. Life was good.

"Mr. Giles was happy. He tossed out some ideas for the next night. I could tell he was fully into this mascot thing already. He had been treading cautiously up 'til then, but once he saw the Phanatic in the flesh, he was totally committed. He said, 'Hey Dave, I got this idea. Why don't you go out with the ground crew when they smooth down the base paths in the fifth inning? Just see what happens.'

"'Just see what happens' comprised the entirety of the Bill Giles' Phillie Phanatic Book of Instructions. Bill was a good baseball man, but his approach might prove lacking in other areas. He would not have been, for example, a good advance scout for General Custer giving similar kinds of advice to the General like, 'Hey, Custer, why not take your entire contingent out to Little Big Horn, kind of hang around out there, and, you know, just see what happens?'"

Dave took Bill's orders-cum-advice about the ground crew.

DAVE RAYMOND: "I went out to third base and pretended to polish it with my tongue. That would be my Phanatic tongue, not my real tongue. After that, I started running the bases and, in the process, colliding one-by-one with the ground crew. It was new to them and totally unrehearsed. They had no idea what I was doing or why, which made us even. But they played along, and pretty much from the get-go, we started to adlib routines. We did it for years."

The ground crew worked out an Unknown Comic routine, mimicking a popular show of the time, *The Gong Show*, conceived and hosted by Philadelphia's own wacky, weird Chuck Barris.

DAVE RAYMOND: "I started to rely on the ground crew as a foil for the Phanatic. We used to put a wig on one of them, and he'd wear a garish blue dress with it. Then he'd hop on top of the dugout as a Surfer Girl and dance with the Phanatic to 'Wipeout.' The fans roared."

The Phillie Phanatic was an overnight hit. Dave Raymond gave the Phanatic personality—in contrast, for instance, to the robotic Mr. Met with his amorphous, flat-liner personality.

DAVE RAYMOND: "The Phils gave me free rein. I just pushed the envelope as far as I could. I cultivated a persona for the Phanatic. He became like the guy who could act out the things the devil inside us tempts us to do but polite society prohibits. Like the Phillie Phanatic could walk up to pretty girls and kiss them. He could rub a bald guy's head for a laugh. He could waddle behind a fat guy and imitate him. He could stand in front of an umpire or an opposing player and heckle them. And it was all understood to be in good fun and everyone, even the victim—or especially the victim—got a chuckle. Or at least they *usually* did. Sometimes I went a little over the top. When I did, I heard about it from the Phillies—believe me. But the Phils and I had this unspoken agreement that if I wasn't on the carpet at least once a week, I wasn't really doing my job."

The Phillie Phanatic's exploits, peccadilloes, and imbroglios are many.

DAVE RAYMOND: "I was at an appearance at a car dealership with Pete Rose who was there to promote his new record, 'The Charlie Hustle.' I got a little carried away. I imitated Pete's head-first slide. Problem was, I slid through the showcase window head first. A lot of people thought it was part of the act, a piece of brilliant showmanship. I thank them for that kind but misplaced vote of confidence. But it wasn't showmanship, and the dealership didn't appreciate it. They called the police. When they arrived, I signed the complaint, 'The Phillie Phanatic.' The police did not appreciate that piece of showmanship, either. Only Pete and I got a kick out of it.

"Another time we were in New York. Now please remember I was young and crazy at that time, and occasionally—only occasionally— exercised bad judgment. Studio 54 was the red-hot 'in' place at the time. I tried to get in just as myself, but the line wrapped around the block. So I went back to the van, put the Phanatic suit on, and they gave me the star treatment. I got right in. To this day, the Phillies don't know about that episode, and maybe a few others."

And Dave, I assure you, they never will.

Dave attributes his success as the Phanatic to the fact that his mother, Suzanne, is deaf. She was a certified teacher of sign language and very active in the deaf community. As a counselor at the Sterck School for the Deaf in Newark, Delaware, she once received Deaf Person of the Year honors for the state of Delaware. Her son's penchant for pantomime, which he did so cleverly as the Phillie Phanatic, owed to years of signing with his mother. Dave's mom often told him that he moved and gestured the same way she taught her deaf students to communicate.

Everybody loved Raymond. But Dave decided to move on in 1994. He joined forces with the Phanatic's creators, Bonnie Erickson and Wayde Harrison, and launched his own enterprise, Acme Mascots. Eventually Dave started his own business, Raymond Entertainment Group. He left a huge legacy as a mascot and a good luck charm. The Phillies were 154 games better than .500 in games where Dave appeared as the Phillie Phanatic. Eat your hearts out, Roberts and Carlton.

Want-Ad

The Phillies still exhibit many of the characteristics of the old-fashioned, pre–Gordon Geckko, family-run corporation, disdainfully dismissed nowadays as "Mom and Pops." The Phil's management style favors Fezziwig over the Marley-Scrooge model. Corporations are actually not people, my friend, and considerations like loyalty and promoting from within do not arrest or adulterate the organization.

When Dave Raymond suited up as the Phanatic for the last time in 1993, he left on a high note. The Phils had just won the 1993 pennant, their first since 1983. They had lost one of the most exciting World Series within memory. They had arguably fired up the city and fan base more than any Philadelphia team in history. They had shattered all previous attendance records and had unquestionably garnered more national attention and recognition than any Phillies team in the organization's 110 years of existence.

But picking the person who would suit up as the next Phillie Phanatic did not go unnoticed in a city that had woven the mascot into its very fabric. The Phils promoted from within, appointing or anointing the irrepressible Tom Burgoyne. He has held the job with panache and pride ever since. Tom's backstory is—well—intriguing. His road to wearing the green furry costume for a living resembles, I surmise, nothing like any you've traveled to land a job.

TOM BURGOYNE: "I was working as a salesman for computer supplies and business forms. I wasn't finding it very stimulating or rewarding. One Sunday I was paging through the want ads in the *Philadelphia*

Inquirer. By pure chance, I saw a want ad: 'Mascots Wanted.' I assumed or hoped it was for a legitimate job and not for something kinky. I'm kidding. Anyway, it said to send a resume to a P.O. Box number in Philly. In high school, I was the Hawk mascot at St. Joseph's Prep. I loved it! The Prep's student newspaper interviewed me when I graduated and asked me the standard high-school question, the same one you hear in job interviews: 'What do you see yourself doing five years from now?' I answered pathetically—er, make that prophetically, 'I'll be the Phillie Phanatic by then!'

"Okay, getting back to the want ad, I sent my resume. I figured I might land something that would give me some extra cash. Everybody likes extra cash, except that baby in the Jimmy Fallon commercials. I thought I could do little gigs like Ronald McDonald or Hamburglar or something like that. I packed the resume with all the typical resume jargon. I had a BA from Drexel, and I had worked for a lot of different companies as a co-op in college. I ended my cover letter with the 'inspired' and 'inspirational' clincher: 'Let me bring your costume to life.'

"A couple weeks later, out of the blue, the Phillies called me saying they were looking for a backup Phillie Phanatic. Dave Raymond was swamped with personal appearances. His backup at the time was headed off to become the mascot for the new NBA basketball franchise in Orlando. So the Phils invited me in for an interview.

"I found myself in a bizarre waiting room—not the room itself, just the humanity that filled it. They gave me a questionnaire. While I was busy filling it out, the guy next to me sized me up and tried to shatter my confidence. He broke the bombshell that he was once the great and powerful Socceroo, a kangaroo mascot for the now-defunct Philadelphia Fever of the professional indoor soccer league. He eyed me up top to bottom, a cigarette stuck in the corner of his mouth. His frame exceeded nature's optimal design by about 15 pounds. He continued, 'Before Socceroo, I was a clown for the circus and McDuff the Crime Dog.'

"Hearing such impressive credentials might have snapped and sapped the confidence of a lesser man. Not I! Undaunted, I completed my questionnaire.

"I sat and waited for my turn. Finally, I was beckoned in. I walked in and found myself facing a panel of four people: Wayde Harrison and Bonnie Erickson—the husband-wife team that designed the Phanatic costume—Chris Long, and Dave Raymond.

"Suffice it to say, this was not your standard corporate interview. In a typical job interview, the applicant doesn't have to field questions like, 'Who's your favorite cartoon character?' and 'What's your favorite comedy movie of all time?' Even giving an answer to such questions might disqualify you in a normal job interview. My answers, by the way, were Bugs Bunny and *Animal House*. The panel was actually taking notes. I got nervous. In this high-stakes, James Bond–like, cat-and-mouse game, was it possible that saying *Animal House* instead of *Caddyshack* might mean the difference between landing the job or losing it to an obviously less qualified applicant? Such a loss could make me hate *Animal House*. Nah, nothing could do that.

"The panel asked me what kind of music I like. That's a no-brainer. Jackson Browne and the Boss, southern rock—I could have gone on and on. They asked if I could dance. I told them I was a regular at the Springfield Inn in Sea Isle City and that I liked to dance at weddings. Then I stopped myself short. I might have been coming across as a barfly who needs a few beers as fuel for his two left feet. Dave Raymond jumped in. 'Can you show us your dance moves?' *Okay, I get it*, I thought. They were looking for the life of the party, the guy with the lampshade on his head. I started looking around for a lampshade. I kid. I asked them, 'Can I take off my shoes?' 'Sure, whatever you want,' Chrissy said. Next thing I know, I had yanked Chrissy away from the table and we were rockin' out to Sam Cooke's 'Twistin' the Night Away' that blasted from a boom box that someone plopped on the table.

"I wasn't intimidated by the panel's comments while I was cutting the rug. 'Hey look at those faces he's making! He'll get more laughs as a headless Phanatic!' That comment turned out to be prophetic, but more on that later.

"When the music stopped, I put my shoes back on, walked back to the table, and fanned out a series of convincing photos. 'Here I am on top of the statue at 15th and Market during the Phillies' 1980 World Series celebration.' Then I flung my prized possession out on the table—a photo of me in a tuxedo with a Julius Erving jersey under my coat, shaking hands with my childhood hero, Dr. J. The picture had run in the *Inquirer* the day after the Doc's last regular season game at the Spectrum when he scorched the Pacers for his 30,000th career point. Then I pulled out all the stops. I played my trump card. I pulled out the St. Joe's interview from six years earlier—the one I mentioned before—the one where I predicted I'd be the Phillie Phanatic five years after I graduated.

"I wrapped up my little photo session by saying, 'So there you have it. Being the Phanatic is my destiny!'

"Chrissy asked me to come back after lunch for the final phase of the interview, which was to audition in the costume. I gulped down lunch and headed back for the fitting. It was snug. I had to wear a lacrosse helmet, which supported the Phanatic head. They buckled me in. I was a bit disoriented. The head rises a good 10" above the lacrosse helmet. But everything else felt the same. Everything else felt normal, except that the suit smelled like a dog that had just come in from the rain. Aside from the discomfort of the roly-poly belly throwing off my gait, having four fingers instead of five, and a feeling that my forehead was about a foot longer than it should be, I was set to rock 'n' roll.

"'Now remember, Tom, when those doors open, you're the Phillie Phanatic,' someone yelled. The doors swung open. 'Hi Phanatic,' Chrissy yelled in a sing-songy lilt. 'This is Anthony. He's videotaping all our Phanatics today.' '*All* our Phanatics!'

"Ouch! What's this, 'All our Phanatics' stuff? I didn't like hearing that, but I couldn't let it get to me.

"Chrissy walked across the room, mimicking a pregnant woman. 'There goes a pregnant woman, Phanatic,' Dave yelled out. I hustled over to the 'pregnant woman,' thrust out my belly, and pantomimed that I could feel the baby kicking. I kicked my leg out and pantomimed 'Twins' by holding up two fingers. Dave came right back with, 'Phanatic! Mike Schmidt just hit a home run!' I broke into that little butt-swivel that Michael Jack did. I swung my arms, looked high off into the distance with my hand over my eyes, visor-like, and strutted, peacock-like, around the room.

"Well, you get the idea. They threw situation after situation at me, duplicating what the Phillie Phanatic faces in unreal life. I don't have the heart to call it real life. I thought I was going to pass out after such a nonstop succession of fake grass drills, pushups, and silly dances. Mercifully, my audition came to an end.

"*So that's what it's like*, I thought. Being the Phanatic is just a nonstop parade of changing situations and ad libbing and endlessly, relentlessly 'being on.' And the Phillie Phanatic gets the added pleasure of doing it all inside an uncomfortable, insulated suit in 100-degree Philly heat! Maybe the job isn't all it's cracked up to be.

"A week later, the phone rang. Chrissy Long shouted, 'Congratulations, Phanatic, you got the job!' I've been the Phanatic now since 1994, and I've got to say—it is all it's cracked up to be. And then some!"

Gift

After landing the backup Phanatic job, Tom Burgoyne served not only in that capacity but also as part-time scoreboard operator and Vet music orchestrator for half a decade. As for becoming the "real" Phanatic, as Burgoyne knew, that might have never happened. Dave Raymond was a popular Phanatic and superb in the role. Dave loved Philly, loved the team, and seemed content to play the Phanatic forever. But nothing lasts forever, and Dave Raymond ceded the mascot suit to Tom Burgoyne in typical Dave Raymond style.

TOM BURGOYNE: "Dave has a flair for the dramatic. You can see it in our wedding video. There was Dave being interviewed at our reception. And what does he do? He does this falling-on-his-sword routine, symbolically acting out the death of himself as the Phanatic. The first time we watched it, my wife, Jen, asked, 'What's he doing?' I said, 'He's giving us the best wedding gift we got. He's turning over the Phanatic role to me!'

"What an incredible ride 1993 was for me personally. The Phils had the most popular team ever that year. They not only went from worst in '92 to first in '93, but they did so with swagger and style. Except for one day, they occupied first place from Day 1 to Day 162. I got married after the season on November 1. We planned a huge bash followed by a trip to Maui.

"In 1993, I was a busy backup Phanatic, really busy. I made over 225 appearances at bar mitzvahs, weddings, cow-milking contests—yes, you read that correctly—birthday parties, and the like. When I first saw our wedding video and caught Dave's act about giving up the Phanatic job, I didn't know how to interpret it. Dave is talented and unpredictable, whether in or out of costume. But shortly after I got back from my honeymoon, there I was one day, eating lunch with him. Dave told me he was moving on and starting his own company. He told me that he had officially recommended me to the Phillies as his replacement. I was gobsmacked! I was in line to get my dream job! Of course, it wasn't a slam-dunk, or as our legendary announcer Whitey Ashburn would have put it, 'It was not a lead-pipe cinch.' The Phillies had to okay it. And of course, I would be under the scrutiny of the Philly press and Philly fans.

"But everything worked out with a few minor speed bumps along the way. Next year, there I was on Opening Day with the U.S. Navy Leapfrog Parachute Team, acting all bright-eyed and bushy-tailed in my green costume. Of course, the Phanatic is always bright-eyed and bushy-tailed. The fans, as always, were great to me. The press was receptive and positive. And we all lived, as the story goes, happily ever after.

"I should add something else about our wedding, which could be a novel in itself. When I popped the question to my future wife, she said, 'Yes.' She had visions of a lovely spring wedding, with flowers in bloom, and a wedding party where all were garbed in spring pastel shades, and an album full of wedding photos taken in some verdant glistening glade. I listened politely as she detailed her reverie. Then I gave her a taste of what life would be like for the wife of the Phillie Phanatic's backup. I said, 'That sounds awesome, but remember I'm a pretty busy guy in the spring. I'm pretty well booked with appearances and games all the way through September.' 'Well,' Jen stammered, 'At least we'll have a lovely September wedding. The flowers will still be gorgeous, the weather warm…' 'But,' I butted in again, 'You see, the Phils have made some good off-season acquisitions who I think are going to plug some holes in the lineup. If everybody stays healthy and the starting rotation gives us some innings and quality starts, we'll be playing some meaningful games this September.' 'Okay,' she conceded. 'Then we'll push it back to early October when we…' I cut in once again, ever so gently, 'Well, you see the playoffs and World Series start in early October. How about we plan for November? What a beautiful month November is! Thanksgiving, the start of the holidays. I love the energy.'

"The way I like to think of it Jen did get her spring wedding, just not spring in our hemisphere."

Headless

It was a dark and rainy night. No, truly it was. I was there. I remember it well. The Phillies were holding their Final Pieces auction. The Vet was soon to be demolished, and memorabilia of all kinds was being auctioned off. The Phillie Phanatic and I had just collaborated on our second book together, *Movin' On Up*, which celebrated the Phillies' move to Citizens Bank Park. The book's theme was an ode to the ascent of the Phillies, the city of Philadelphia, as well as numerous expatriate Phillie fans.

Anyway, for several hours on that particular evening Friday, February 6, 2004, Tom Burgoyne and I sat and signed books for the Phillie faithful as they swept through the Spectrum, hunting for memorabilia.

Tom got up and down several times from the book-signing table. His evening was his typical Phanatic marathon of donning and doffing his costume. He was signing a book one minute as Tom Burgoyne and the next minute creating havoc as the Phanatic Phanatic.

As the hour grew late and we each tired of sitting there signing books, Tom said to me, "Randy Wolf and L.A. [Larry Andersen] are going

Opening Day Performers

1971—Helicopter ball drop to Coach Mike Ryan
1972—Kiteman I
1973—Kiteman II
1974—Cannonball Man
1975—High-wire motorcycle act
1976—Paul Revere delivers the ball to Rocketman
1977—Parachutist delivers the ball
1978—Parachutist delivers the ball
1979—Golden Knights Parachute Team
1980—Kiteman III
1981—Helicopter ball drop to Coach Mike Ryan
1982—Slide for Life ball delivery
1983—Parachutist Jim O'Brien
1984—Cannonball Man
1985—Starship III
1986—Wondrous Winns High-Wire Act
1987—Rocketman [crashed in practice]
1988—Lost Ball Contest
1989—Rainout
1990—Kiteman IV
1991—Phanatic throws the ball from the roof to Mike Ryan
1992—Benny the Bomb
1993—US Navy Leap Frog Parachute Team
1994—US Navy Leap Frog Parachute Team
1995—Helicopter drop to Mike Ryan and Kiteman V
1996—Phanatic throws ball from the lift in front of Phanavision (Leap
     Frogs could not jump because of excessive wind)
1997—Magic act with Phanatic appearing out of inflated baseball
1998—Phanatic Slide for Life
1999—Rocketman to Kiteman to Handman (man with hand transplant)
2000—Mission to Mars
2001—Navy Leap Frogs

onstage soon for an interview. I'm gonna go down and cause some havoc. Wanna wrap it up and join me?"

I was tired and had a long drive home, so I declined. Then Tom took off to find the footlights, and I took off to find the sky that was dumping buckets of water. It was not a pleasant evening.

Next morning, the phone rang bright and early. It was Tom. "You're not going to believe what happened," he said. "Somebody stole my head! When we left the table last night and Christine [the Phanatic's support team] and I went back to the [makeshift] Spectrum dressing room I was using, the head was gone!"

He didn't have any more details. "Just keep it under your hat," Tom said. "The Phillies are keeping this one under wraps."

I hung up and kept mum—until Monday when I spent the morning hours fielding phone calls asking, "Hey what's up with the Phanatic's head?" It soon became apparent that I was the only one in the city who was keeping mum. The story was all over the local news. Angelo Cataldi and the WIP radio morning crew kept calling Tom's house on Monday morning, pestering him about the whereabouts of the head. They even had the audacity to suggest it might be a publicity stunt for *Movin' On Up*. We were incensed—not at the accusation but that we hadn't thought of that gimmick ourselves. Monday's *Philadelphia Daily News* ran a huge photo of a Phanatic, whose head had been digitally removed, dancing on the dugout.

The whole world was making hay of the heist. Shock jock Howard Stern announced on his nationally syndicated radio program that one of his sponsors, Gary Barbera Dodge, was offering a $5,000 reward. For Stern to interrupt his continuous coverage of strippers, midgets, and other earthly delights to hunt for the head was humbling yet consistent with his program's standard sterling content.

Not wanting to miss the chance to cash in on a boffo publicity opportunity, WIP asked to "borrow" the head of the backup Phanatic. They planned to prop it up on the back of a flatbed and parade it around the city, asking Philadelphia's fine citizens if they "had seen anything resembling this creature in recent days." Somehow, the Phillies organization didn't share WIP's enthusiasm and nixed the idea.

The *Philadelphia Daily News* offered a $1,000 reward for information leading to the head's return. Another local radio station, WLDW, also offered a $5,000 reward. They even conducted a candlelight vigil in their parking lot. The ceremony was billed as a "prayer service."

By the following Saturday, even Jimmy Fallon on *Saturday Night Live*'s "Weekend Update" was chiming in. He did a blurb announcing that the world-famous Phillie Phanatic's head was stolen during a charity event. Fallon deadpanned that the Philadelphia police were on the case tracking several leads—at which point, a doctored photo of a guy wearing a business suit with the Phanatic's head on top popped up on the screen next to Fallon.

"Police believe *this* man may be a suspect," Fallon concluded.

Unbeknownst to him, Jimmy Fallon nailed it. The Philadelphia police were on the case. They were finding little humor in the folly. Instead they felt the pressure of the national press corps making light of the department just for the yuks.

TOM BURGOYNE: "Three cops came into our brand-new offices at Citizens Bank Park to take my statement and reenact the events of the night in question. I accompanied them when they checked all the doors and exits that the thief might have used. They got a list of all the people who registered for the auction, figuring the thief might be on it. They checked Comcast SportsNet's tapes. Comcast had taped a 'Meet the Phillies' segment that evening, and they were hoping it might reveal something. They checked the surveillance tapes at the Wachovia Center. I trailed along everywhere with them.

"Wachovia's security staff was all over the caper. They handed the cops and me a black-and-white photo of a lone man in the hallway just behind the room where I changed. 'That's your man,' they said.

"We all gathered around a bank of security monitors in the control room and studied tapes taken by the ticket window. We watched a heavy-set guy enter the lobby, walk up toward the ticket office, and then veer off, slipping behind a door marked 'Authorized Personnel Only.'

"'Gotcha now,' said one of the cops. 'He just upped the charge from theft to burglary!' The next shot we watched was from a camera outside the break room. It was 6:55 PM, and the perpetrator was walking toward the surveillance camera. Suddenly, he disappeared from view. For the next three minutes, the hallway was empty. Then he reappeared and there it was—the Phanatic's head barely visible under his now-bulging jacket.

"The police now had the smoking gun. They were set to post the photos and the footage on every area Crime Fighter broadcast. But that never came about. Unexpectedly, the thief made a call to WYSP, the Philly radio station affiliated at the time with Howard Stern. The DJ was Philly's legendary rocker Tommy Conwell of Tommy Conwell and the Young Rumblers. Tommy was skeptical when the guy confessed. The station had received several crank calls after posting the $5,000 reward. But, after instructing the caller to bring it in to the station, an hour or so later, there was the culprit walking through the lobby at 5th and Market with the Phanatic's head in hand.

"Since the whole city was on red alert for the Phanatic's head, a guy in the lobby saw the head and called the precinct. Within minutes the place was swarming with detectives who rushed up to the studio and arrested the guy.

"At the police station, the guy didn't come clean at first. He hemmed and hawed. He claimed his kids found the head while sledding—an obvious snow job since there wasn't a flake of snow to be found from Philly right on up to the Poconos. Eventually, he admitted he had been at the auction. He said he saw two kids in the parking lot carrying the Phanatic's head. He chose to do his civic duty and confronted them. They dropped the head and ran. He then picked it up and ran.

"Finally, the guy came clean. He said he just wasn't thinking. He stumbled upon the head and, like many things in life, keeping it seemed like a good idea at the time.

"While that interrogation was going on, I was having quite a heady, so to speak, conversation with the Phillies' brass, agonizing over what to say at the press conference. Someone suggested that the police present me with the Phanatic's head. *Nahhhh!* For years we've been taking great pains *not* to show Dave or me in the process of donning the Phanatic costume. We've 'trained' the media to refer to me—and Dave before me—as the 'best friend' of the Phanatic.

"What we landed on was having the cops pull up to the press conference at the Phillies Preview Center. With the Phanatic's head concealed in a trash bag, they would walk past the jungle of cameras and microphones and enter the building. A few minutes later—bingo!—out would come the Phanatic, head and all.

"But the best-laid plans—well, you know how that goes. My cell phone rang right before the planned press conference. It was Detective Stephen Caputo calling from the interrogation room. 'Tom, the guy just confessed. He's writing down his statement right now. We've got an hour of paperwork to clean up, so we can't be at the press conference.'

"As the saying goes, 'The show and/or press conference must go on!' It did, *sans les gendarmes*. At the conference, Tommy Conwell and the other WYSP reps talked about how proud they were that they were the ones who cracked the case and reunited the Phanatic with his head. When my turn at the mic came, I thanked the Philadelphia police department for their efforts and the fans for their support. I closed with, 'Now the Phanatic can get back to the serious business of making a fool of himself.'

"That *should* be the end of the story. It wasn't. I figured I could easily slip away after the press conference and reclaim my head. But when I drove up to the police station, I came upon a sea of cameras and news trucks. As it turns out, the police had scheduled their own press conference. They wanted to announce that their suspect confessed.

"I double-parked my Phanatic van a block or so away from the crowd. I furtively made my way into the station, filled out some forms, and reclaimed the stolen head. The detectives led me down a back staircase that opened onto the street. I headed out with the head in a bag slung over my shoulder. I pulled the visor of my Phillies cap down over my face and hustled past the reporters. I almost made it unnoticed. But suddenly I heard, 'Hey that's Tom! Hey Tom, hold up! He's got the head! Let's see it!'

"I underwent a sudden episode of deafness—nonmedical deafness that used to strike me intermittently as a kid, like when my parents told me to clean my room. I stepped up my pace, opened the van's side door, tossed in the head, and hopped into the driver's seat. In a blink, the cameramen and reporters had caught up. They surrounded the van, demanding a shot of the green, furry head. I rolled down the window, gave the thumbs up sign, whooped up a little 'Go Phillies' chant and pulled away. The cameramen jogged alongside of the van as long as they could. But soon I was outta there, riding free with the fully integrated Phanatic.

"As fate would have it, I had an appearance scheduled that night at Dave and Buster's, the mega-entertainment and restaurant complex on the Delaware River. They were celebrating their 10th anniversary in Philadelphia. When I got there, the TV lights blinded me. Every station had sent a crew to cover the Phanatic's return. I walked in and got swarmed by Mummers who broke into 'Happy Days Are Here Again.' A Ben Franklin look-alike was there high-fiving me—the high-five being a popular form of expression in colonial times. Harry Kalas was there, trumpeting, 'The Phillie Phanatic has his head back!'"

Indeed.

chapter 8

1980

Boo

Pete Rose, never one to duck praise, once said, "Mike Schmidt was the best player in the league three or four days a week when I got to Philadelphia. By the time I left, he had learned to be the best seven days a week."

Michael Jack Schmidt's performance seconds that emotion. During Rose's tenure as a Phil (1979–83), Schmidt reached career highs in single-season batting average (.316), home runs (48), RBIs (121), and slugging percentage (.644). "Rose made the difference," Schmidt acknowledged.

Mike Schmidt's career wasn't all Hall of Fame glory. He endured some hard knocks before rising to the top of his craft.

WHITEY ASHBURN: "Schmidt used to drive me crazy when he came up! He could not handle the breaking ball. At all. He could jump all over a fastball. But he was out of his league on a good breaking ball. To his credit, he adjusted. He learned to hit it, and that's when his star started to rise."

The Phils drafted Schmidt out of Ohio University in the second round of the 1971 amateur draft. He made his MLB debut on September 12 the following year. Four days later, he tagged Montreal Expo pitcher Balor Moore for a seventh-inning three-run homer. It was the first of what became a career total of 548. Schmitty hit that first one in style. It was not only a game-winning hit that accounted for all his team's runs—it was the first run Moore had allowed in his 25 innings of work. Balor's scoreless streak was tops for any pitcher in Montreal's truncated history.

WHITEY ASHBURN: "Balor Moore was only a fair pitcher, but he had that one unhittable stretch. Along comes this kid—how old was Schmitty at the time? 21? 22? And he hits a big homer to snap the streak.

"The press was looking for any ray of hope besides Carlton in 1972. They swarmed Schmidt after the game. They were in for a shock. They weren't used to anyone like Schmitty. They never did get used to him. He had that air of aloofness even as a kid, but he needed seasoning on how to handle the press. Anyway, Schmidt tells them he considers himself a power hitter, and that kind of gave them a storyline to feed on."

It was also probably Schmitty's first-ever comment on hitting philosophy in a career that would be laden with them. In compliance with baseball's unspoken protocol, most ball players in that era restricted their comments to clichéd drivel. Only someone who had made the grade was entitled to wax philosophic on the art of hitting a baseball. Schmidt's comment that day was unusually astute, "I consider myself a power hitter in the sense that I don't have to get all of a pitch to hit it out of the park." But some members of the press felt he had not earned sufficient stripes to declare himself a power hitter.

The press wasn't used to cerebral responses. Throughout his career, Schmidt made a habit of pondering baseball's imponderables, and his responses took provocative detours on occasion from the accepted list of clichés. At the time, Schmidt was in the vanguard of a more frank tell-it-like-it-is generation. The press often mistook his frankness for brashness.

WHITEY ASHBURN: "Schmitty probably wouldn't remember, but I dropped a lot of hints about toning his responses down. The press in this town can make life tough on you. But Schmitty always opted to figure things out for himself. And all in all, I'd have to say, he did just fine doing it his way."

The following year, Schmitty was the Phils' starting third sacker. His rookie season was forgettable and at times painful. In 132 games and 367 at-bats, he slammed 18 HRs. That was the good news. The bad news was that he hit .196 with 136 whiffs. He struck out in 37 percent of his at-bats.

Mike Schmidt watches his third-inning home run against the Atlanta Braves on Friday, July 26, 1980, in Philadelphia. It was Schmidt's second home run of the night, and he later added a double and was walked in the 12th inning to force in the winning run. *(AP Photo)*

JOHN VUKOVICH: "You could see as soon as Schmitty came up he was a power hitter, so what he told the press was true. He had a short, compact swing that you can't teach. You either have it or you don't. I didn't. But I'll tell you what I have that no one else has. I've got some sort of baseball record. I just haven't figured out what to call it. But I'll bet I'm the only guy in history who ever lost his starting job twice, and I lost it both times to a future Hall of Famer. Mike Schmidt took my starting job for the Phillies, and Pete Rose took it at Cincinnati. Ain't no shame in any of that!"

The analytical Schmidt straightened out his freshman hitches and glitches. He blossomed into an All-Star his sophomore season. He also placed sixth in the MVP Award voting and won his first of eight NL home run crowns. On the negative side of the ledger, he led the league in strikeouts—a dubious achievement he would claim, or perhaps it would claim him, four times in his 18-year career. And therein—those whiffs, not his aloofness or unpopular response—lies the heart and heat of what kept the boobirds booing at Mike Schmidt for so long.

WHITEY ASHBURN: "I got a chance to see our two biggest boobird targets: Schmitty and Del Ennis. I played with Del. They booed him unmercifully. People here just don't like power hitters because they strike out a lot. But that's what power hitters do. It might hurt them with the fans, but not in the pocketbook. In my day, we had a saying, 'Home run hitters drive Cadillacs. Singles hitters drive Chevys.' I drove a lot of Chevys in my playing days."

Ashburn wasn't quite correct. Del Ennis actually did *not* strike out much. His highest strikeout total for a single season was 65. That happened in 1946, his rookie year, in which he batted .313 in 540 at-bats. That's a strikeout rate of 12 percent, or 12 strikeouts each 100 at-bats. In Schmidt's worst year for Ks, he struck out 180 times in 562 at-bats or 32 percent of the time. That's almost three times as often as Ennis. It meant boobirds could boo it up every third time Schmitty came up—and sat down. So if not for striking out, why was Schmidt's precursor lustily booed? Liz Ennis, Del's widow, once offered me her thoughts.

LIZ ENNIS: "Years ago, Stu, an old friend of ours, told us that back in the forties and fifties, a lot of gambling took place in the stands during games. Gamblers would bet on anything and everything during the game. They'd bet whether somebody would strikeout or walk, or what inning a pitcher would get knocked out, or how many runs the Phils would score in a certain inning—things like that. Stu said guys who bet on Del to hit a homer would get angry when he didn't and they'd boo him. Del was a hometown boy, so they expected more of him. They expected him to be the next Babe Ruth. So their displeasure for him was amplified, and the whole stadium would pick up on the booing."

The booing became institutionalized in both Schmidt's and Ennis' case. It became a Philly "thing." When you went to the stadium, you bought some beer and hot dogs and booed Ennis or Schmidt.

WHITEY ASHBURN: "I think that could be true. Booing Del and Schmitty wasn't so much dislike or disapproval. It was just something you did when you were at the ball yard."

LIZ ENNIS: "Some people say Del was booed because of city neighborhood rivalries. Neighborhood rivalries were huge in Philadelphia. High school teams, ethnic neighborhoods—they were big rivalries. Del was from Crescentville in the Olney section, and over the years people have told me that fans from rival neighborhoods around the city used to boo Del.

"Eventually the Phils traded Del to St. Louis. The fans there appreciated him. He didn't get booed. In his first year in St. Louis, he roomed with Stan Musial and drove in more runs than Stan. I think the booing bothered Del even more once he experienced such a warm reception in St. Louis. Philly was Del's hometown, and he wanted Philadelphia to like him. He never understood the booing. What fans don't know is that it hurt him very deeply."

As for Schmitty, when the Phillies got more successful in the late seventies, the chorus of Schmidt boos increased out of frustration with his team. The Phils, despite two 101-win seasons—MLB's highest win total each year—failed every postseason until 1980. It all came together

Tribute

On May 26, 1990, the Philadelphia Phillies retired Mike Schmidt's jersey No. 20. Schmidt had long since made peace with the boobirds. Here is an excerpt from his Tribute Night speech on May 26, 1990:

"I'm thankful to baseball for many things. Perhaps the most important are the friendships it has given me. Playing baseball involves living with other players day in and day out—getting to know them, to learn from them, to lean on them in tough times, to survive together. I feel blessed to have made so many true friends in my 17 years of wearing the Phillies uniform. The uniform of a first-class organization headed throughout my career by two first-class men: Ruly Carpenter and Bill Giles. I'm proud to call them both my friends. At times I admit I can be a hard guy to get to know. This makes me even more grateful to those who invested their time and their trust to build a friendship with me. Each of you has my friendship forever.

"And finally, my fans:

"I want to tell you straight from the heart how I feel about you and your influence on this game. As athletes, we're disciplined, we're focused, we're even tough. But I know of no athlete who is immune to fan reaction, positive or negative. Yes, you fans affect the game in a big way. Calling

---

for Schmitty that year. He won the MVP and the World Series MVP, and Philadelphia fans finally realized there was an all-time great in their midst—a rarity in Philadelphia not seen since the heyday of Robin Roberts. And fans started focusing on the voluminous good stuff Schmidt did. Tolerance increased for his strikeouts, and the boos died down.

In the latter stages of his career, Schmidt cut down on strikeouts significantly. In his final two productive seasons, he struck out less than 100 times per year. His batting average was .290 and .293, respectively. In both years, his home run total exceeded 35. As Ashburn posited, Schmidt had achieved his goal and developed into a complete hitter.

Philadelphia fans spectators hardly describes your impact. You help mold the spirit of a team. Your positive feedback is crucial in the Phillies' fight to stay on top. You know, I'm often asked what I miss most about the game. It's tough to sort out all the wonderful memories and come up with a definite answer. But I can tell you this; I'll always miss the goosebumps I got when you cheered me. I've collected 18 years of those goosebumps, from my first hit back in 1972 to the welcome you gave me tonight. To right now. That feeling can never be recreated, but that feeling will always be remembered.

"My dreams started on a small playground near my home where I first learned how to hold a bat. My dreams came true here on this field. This game—baseball—is rich with strategy, talent, challenge, excitement, and yes, tradition. But most of all, this game of baseball creates a bond—an indescribable bond, a bond that brings all of us together. All of us not only teams but families, friends, communities, and yes, even countries. At this very moment, I feel that bond and it will always be with me. I don't know where life will lead, but the Phillies and Philadelphia will forever hold a very special place in my heart.

"Thank you all—all of you."

ASHBURN: "Complete hitters don't get booed as much by the fans. The cheers are louder for the big bombers, but so are boos. I still think the best thing Schmitty did to stop the boobirds was to cut down on the strikeouts."

Bumps

Stephen Colbert insists that political candidates need the "Colbert Bump" to win. In 1980, the Phils needed a healthy "Bystrom Bump" to win their first World Championship.

It's true. Sometimes teams, even great teams, need a bump to get over the hump. They need heroics from an unexpected source.

One of baseball's fabled "bumps" came in 1957. A great Milwaukee team was anchored by first-tier Hall of Famers Henry Aaron, Warren Spahn, and Eddie Mathews along with second-tier Hall of Famer Red Schoendienst—bolstered by a big-name cast that included Joe Adcock, Del Crandall, Bill Bruton, Lew Burdette, Bob Buhl, and Johnny Logan. Despite such star power, the Braves had to turn to an unheralded rookie to provide the bump they needed to secure first place.

The Braves languished in third place as late as mid-July. Then Bob "Hurricane" Hazle—nicknamed for the hurricane that devastated the East Coast in 1954—was brought up to the Braves in late July. He gave the Braves the bump needed to vault over the competition. In less than three weeks, from August 9 through August 25, Hazle batted .565 (that's a hit more than every other at-bat) with five home runs and 19 RBIs in 14 games. In a crucial August 9–11 series against the Braves' main rivals, the Cardinals, Hazle blasted seven hits and five RBIs that led to a Braves sweep. The Hurricane continued his surge, batting .556 in his first dozen games. He closed the season with a glitzy .403 average, seven HR, and 27 RBIs in 155 plate appearances. For good measure, on the next-to-last day of the season, Hazle broke up a no-hit bid by Cincinnati's Johnny Klippstein with a two-out, eighth-inning single.

Marty Bystrom's 1980 Bystrom Bump for the Phils was arguably just as impressive and important. He was brought up in September after an injury to starter Nino Espinosa. Bystrom's first mound appearance was a mop-up role. The Phils were down 6–0 to the Dodgers when Marty entered in the eighth inning. He didn't give up a hit, but the contest was already lost 6–0.

The Phils were in second place at the time. They were sinking. The loss was the Phils' third straight loss to the Dodgers, who had been their '77 and '78 nemesis. Moreover, two of those losses were shut-outs. The Phils' sole victory came from another notable 1980 rookie, Bob Walk.

Three days after his Dodgers debut, 22-year-old Marty Bystrom (he had just turned 22 at the end of July) was on the hill against the Mets.

The Phils had somewhat righted themselves after the L.A. meltdown by sweeping a short two-game series against the Pirates. Their play was still shaky. It took a 14th-inning sacrifice bunt by Bob Boone to win the getaway game in the Pirates' series. Nonetheless, the win put them a half-game behind the front-running Montreal Expos.

MARTY BYSTROM: "Like any rookie, I was nervous. I don't know if I'd have been less nervous if the game weren't so crucial, but I did get into a good rhythm pretty fast. The '80 Phils were a solid team with Mike Schmidt, Pete Rose, Steve Carlton, Boonie [Bob Boone], Larry Bowa, the Bull [Greg Luzinski], and a ton of other talent. They had missed several opportunities in the late seventies to win a pennant, and they were determined to get it right this year."

Bystrom twirled a complete game, five-hit shutout.

MARTY BYSTROM: "I went up against Mark Bomback. Our guys made things easy for me. We put up a three-spot in the first inning before the Mets even batted. In the first inning, Frank Taveras got the first hit I ever gave up. Then he stole second. But I got out of the inning. After that, the game settled into a rhythm. They didn't score, and we didn't either until late in the game when we added a few insurance runs. I remember that because I got my first MLB hit in the ninth inning. Then I scored my first run."

JERRY MARTIN, Phillies super-sub: "All the guys were impressed with Marty. He gave the team a lift, that's for sure. When fresh talent shows up at the end of a long campaign, you'd better believe that lifts a team—and even more so if it's a pitcher who shows up. Pitchers wear down over the course of a long season. A fresh arm makes a huge difference down the stretch in a tight pennant race. Marty fit the bill. Getting a shutout in a crucial game when we were making our move for first place really boosted morale."

Bystrom's coolness under fire earned him a spot in a now-tired Phils' rotation. In Marty's second appearance, he pitched a Sunday getaway game against the Cards on the heels of a nifty 2–1 Carlton win the night before.

MARTY BYSTROM: "I had great support that day. We jumped out early again. [The Phils plated six in the third for a 7–0 lead.] I'm proud to say I had a shutdown inning right after that. You can't put too high a premium on shutdown innings. They keep momentum on your side.

"Anyway, I left the game in the seventh with a shutout. After I left, the Cards made some noise, but we were never really in trouble, especially with the Phils fans backing us. At that point in the season, the Philly fans were starting to feel another division title coming our way. Their support gave us a great boost."

At that juncture, Marty was 2–0 with a 0.00 ERA. Those two wins were crucial. The Expos kept on winning and still held a one-game lead. The following Saturday, manager Dallas Green again handed the ball to Bystrom—this time against the Cubs in Chicago.

MARTY BYSTROM: "Schmitty parked one in the first. No story there. He loved Wrigley Field. He'd have broken every home run record in existence if he played his whole career in Chicago. Anyway, we jumped out again in the first. They were spoiling me with those first-inning scores! I was going great. I had a 4–0 lead until their big bomber, Dave Kingman, hit one out in the fourth. I held on, though. I got into trouble in the middle innings, so Dallas yanked me. Kevin Saucier came in, threw a double-play ball, and shut them down. We went on to win."

Ramon Aviles, a lesser light on the 1980 Phils, underscored Bystrom's impact.

RAMON AVILES: "I don't know why, but it seemed like every time Marty pitched, I got a start! I would spell Bowa or Trillo in the middle infield. I remember that game in Chicago because I doubled in a run in an important game. I was so happy to contribute. We were really gaining momentum at that point, and Marty had so much to do with that."

Again the Phils' young rookie gave the team a huge boost to keep them snapping at the heels of a hot, determined Expos team that tenaciously clung to a 1½-game lead. The next time he took the hill, Bystrom launched the Phils back into first place, twirling a 2–1 gem against the Mets. No early support this time—the contest was deadlocked at zero until a leadoff Manny Trillo triple resulted in a two-run Phillies fifth. Marty held New York scoreless before finally surrendering a run in the eighth and getting some relief help from Dickie Noles. The score remained 2–1 the rest of the way, and the Phils found themselves back in first place.

Two days after Bystrom's win, Steve Carlton and Bob Walk dropped back-to-back games against the Expos, who surged back into first place. The Phils then peeled off four straight Ws against the Cubs at the Vet. Bystrom authored the second, a 14–2 laugher that turned out to be his final regular season appearance.

Marty Bystrom finished the 1980 campaign with a glittering 5–0, 1.50 ERA line, registered in its entirety at the peak of crunch time. To his crucial regular season contribution he tacked on a stellar performance in the National League Championship Series, which many consider the greatest NLCS in history. In the fifth and deciding game of the series, it was 22 year-old Marty Bystrom who Dallas Green sent to the hill.

MARTY BYSTROM: "What a thrill! What a responsibility! Like the rest of the club, I was determined, that we were *not* going to lose this game and this series—not when we fought so hard to get here. I went up against Nolan Ryan, who was already a huge legend—a guaranteed Hall of Famer. But I had confidence. I had decent stuff that day, and I had a great and determined Phillies team behind me."

The Astros jumped to an early lead when Jose Cruz double-plated Terry Puhl for a 1–0 Astros advantage in the first. Thanks to a two-run Bob Boone safety, the Phils moved ahead 2–1 in the second. In the sixth, Luzinski muffed Denny Walling's liner to left-center field. Alan Ashby singled to score Walling with an unearned run that tied the contest 2–2. Green yanked Bystrom. The Phils went on to win an unforgettably wild and wooly seesaw contest that saw the Phils flip-flop a 5–2 deficit into a 7–5 advantage in the top of the eighth only to have the Astros tie them 7–7 in the bottom half of the inning.

Knotted after regulation, the game went into extra innings. In the 10th, a Garry Maddox double produced an 8–7 Phillies lead. Dick

Ruthven held on to it, and the Phillies headed to their first World Series in 30 years.

RICHIE ASHBURN: "They were probably the most exciting times I've ever seen in baseball. The team was equal to every challenge, and Marty Bystrom's role—well, you can't put too much importance on it. Without Bystrom's September, the Phillies don't win. I played against 'Hurricane' Hazle. The Braves were a great team, but without Hazle, the Braves wouldn't have won, even with all their Hall of Famers. Yep, I saw them both, Hazle and Bystrom, and I think Marty gave the Phils more of a boost than Hazle gave the Braves."

Victory

On June 16, 2000, I caught up with the 1980 Phils again, 20 years after the glory of their times. Most of the team, except for Pete Rose, came home for the reunion. The Phils arranged a special Memory Lane Gala— a long cocktail party for everyone to reconnect. The Gala was followed by an Academy of Music performance, highlighted by Tug McGraw's (overly) dramatic reading of "Casey at the Bat" and dinner at the now-defunct Toto's across the street.

The evening afforded lots of time to chill out and filter the past through the prism of time. To a man, the players on the 1980 squad pinned the last inning in Game 6 of the World Series and the subsequent victory celebration as the emotional highpoint of a rigorous up-and-down season. To most, it was the emotional high of their lives. And universally, the '80 edition of Philly's boys of summer continues to marvel at the incredible outpouring of appreciation and love that gushed their way from fans whose hopes had been dashed season after season for almost a century.

Millions of fans in Phillies Nation conflate the final inning with the victory celebration. Tug McGraw did not. The Tugger felt like the victory celebration was a distant dream as he strode out to the mound to replace Steve Carlton in the historic Game 6 of the World Series. Sure, when Tug took over the Phils held a comfortable 4–0 lead. Sure, Lefty had walked the leadoff man, John Wathan, and sure enough, Carlton had surrendered a single to Jose Cardenal. But hey, Tugger was coming in and, in the minds of 65,838 screaming out-of-their-minds fans at the Vet, the outcome was, as announcer Whitey Ashburn used to say, "a lead-pipe cinch."

Why? Because despite being in a position that no fan had ever savored in 97 seasons of Phillies baseball (i.e., seeing their heroes six outs away from a World Series championship), the 1980 Phillies Nation knew the game was being placed in the secure hands of their lights-out warrior, the game-over overlord, the rollicking rogue who spit in the eye of danger. So what if Carlton got himself in a little jam? No worry! The Phils' young Lochinvar—well okay, more like a middle-aging Lochinvar—had come out of the west, bustling toward the mound, slapping his glove against his thigh, quick-stepping up to his dome-of-dirt throne, brimming with confidence. And everybody in Philly was thinking the same thought, "Turn out the lights. The party's over."

Tug McGraw was the soul of the 1980 squad. Years earlier, Tug was the guy who had fired up the '73 Mets with his mantra, "You gotta' believe!" And 1980 was his glorious encore.

TUG MCGRAW: "That 1973 Mets season was amazing even though Casey [Stengel, the Mets' first manager] was gone and we were no longer 'The Amazins!' Did you know we were in last place at the end of August? Remember that? I know we were because on the last day of August, I won a game in relief that finally got us out of the basement. Then we got hot.... I got hot! I could just feel everything turning. It was all going our way. Something special was happening, and I knew we were gonna ride that wave all the way to a flag. I started telling anyone who'd listen, 'You gotta believe!' Well, you gotta believe it didn't take long until our whole team started to believe. And we did ride that thing all the way to a flag."

Tug was right. That September, Tug flipped an old saw about March around. He and his Mets went into September like a lamb and came out like a lion. Tug entered the month with a 2–6, 5.05 ERA line. For the rest of the campaign, he went 3–0 with 10 saves and a sensational 0.57 ERA. He continued his mastery, pitching five shutout innings against the

Big Red Machine in the NLCS before appearing in five of seven World Series games.

Tug cooled off the following year, with a poor 6–11, 4.16 ERA season. At season's end, he was shipped off to Philly for Mac Scarce, Del Unser, and John Stearns.

McGRAW: "Turned out to be a good move for me. First of all, I came to Philly. I love Philly fans, although I gotta admit, I loved Mets fans, too. Phils and Mets fans are like peas in a pod. They both love their teams to death. But, when we [the Mets] won the East Division in '73, that turned out to be the only year in the whole decade that Pittsburgh or Philly didn't win the East. So I was in the right place at the right time for almost the whole decade of the seventies. Oh, and don't forget I was part of the Miracle Mets in '69. In fact, if you want to get Lefty [Carlton] started, ask him who got the win in '69 when Lefty struck out 19 Mets and lost the game. Yes, it was the Tugger! The Mets were on fire at that point. A couple of weeks later, Lefty was the one we beat again to clinch the Division. I remember all that stuff, not so much to get under Lefty's skin—although that's kind of fun, too—but because any time you beat Lefty, it's a big deal."

But none of that history was as big a deal as the history that could be made on a chilly October 21. Once again, Lefty and the Tugger were the principles. But this time they wore the same uniform. And this time they were hell-bent and determined to change the history of a proud city, striving for an elusive first—an embarrassing first. Among the teams that existed when the first World Series was played in 1903, Philadelphia was the only franchise that had never won a World Series. And at that crucial juncture in the game, everyone in Philly figured, *Who better than the Tugger to pin all your hopes on?*

Tug had been terrific all season. He finished with 57 appearances, a 5–4 record, and a 1.47 ERA. More important, he had been scalding hot down the stretch, winning five games and picking up five saves in the final month of regular season play. So, this assignment—two on, none out, four-run lead—was a piece of cake. Right, Tug?

McGRAW: "I was running on empty. I was gassed! I may have looked confident, but I don't know what I was feeling inside. I was so excited! When I struck Willie Wilson out, I did it with my 'Peggy Lee' fastball. That's the pitch that makes batters say, 'Is that all there is?'" ("Is That All There Is?" was a popular song recorded by Peggy Lee in 1969.)

The eighth-inning mess that Tug inherited didn't explode. The Royals only managed one run. After the Phils went down 1-2-3 (Maddox, Trillo, Bowa) in their half of the eighth, the Phils still held a 4–1 edge. When Tug took the mound for the top of the ninth, the Phils were only three outs away from their first world championship.

McGRAW: "I had no idea how I was going to get those three outs. I only knew that somehow I was going to do it. When I struck Amos Otis out to open the inning, I thought, *Hey, I can pull this thing off after all!* But it never goes that easy, does it? Next thing I know, the bases are loaded after I walked Willie Mays Aiken and gave up singles to Wathan and Cardenal. That's when something from above must have intervened on that pop-fly that Rose caught. I couldn't believe it! What a boost it gave me. It was 'You gotta believe time' for me all over again!"

"That pop-fly" Tug refers to is the most famous catch of a pop-fly in World Series history, rivaled only by the Billy Martin catch of Jackie Robinson's pop-up in the 1952 World Series. Normally pop-ups are automatic outs, gimmes, no sweat. But if they're dropped, missed, or booted—destinies change. History alters its course.

In the '80 Series, however, with the Phils two outs away from a championship, the Royals were lighting the fuse on Philadelphia's eve of destruction. With the bases loaded, Frank White hit a ball skyward over the right-field dugout. A collective gasp of relief flew out across the Vet as both catcher Bob Boone and first baseman Pete Rose converged on it. The relief turned to horror when Boonie reached for it, and the ball bounced off his glove. Rose, the paragon of heads-up baseball, caught the ball on its descent to save the day. However, Bob Boone, when he recounted the episode 20 years later, had a different, albeit good-natured, take.

BOB BOONE: "Catchers are supposed to handle pop-ups in front of them, behind them, and anywhere else nearby to the right or left. Any place else, the pop-up is the responsibility of the first or third baseman. The play's easier for them. The ball's in front of them, and their glove is better designed to catch it.

"When [Frank] White popped that one up, I knew right away it wasn't my ball. It was too far down the first-base line. But I still have to pursue in case the first baseman trips or boots the ball. But when I reached the end of the dugout, I didn't hear Pete. The whole time the ball was in the air I was expecting him to crash into me and the ball would hit the ground. Finally, since I didn't hear Pete calling for it, I had to do something. I figured I'd better grab for it. So I did. But the ball popped out of my glove. Stabbing for the ball, I was off balance so it was like trying to catch a ball with a wooden board. In that instant, there was so much swirling in my head! I was thinking, *I've never dropped a ball like this in my life! What is going on?* But I never thought it was my ball. Plus, I was expecting a big collision.

"So after the ball pops out of my glove, Pete stabs for the ball and makes the catch. At first I wanted to kill him! It was his ball to begin with! Then when he caught it, I wanted to kiss him. So whenever you writers ask me about that great play Charley Hustle made—and I get asked about it all the time—I say, 'Charley Hustle, my ass! I was the one that hustled for it!'"

McGRAW: "That catch was enough for me! My adrenalin was pumping! And I got a great assist from the Philadelphia Police Department. Mounted Police and police dogs were everywhere I looked, bordering the entire field of play. I honestly think that's the reason manager Dallas Green didn't yank me. He was afraid to go out on the field with those dogs breathing down his neck. He just figured, 'You're on your own now!'"

DICKIE NOLES, Phils relief pitcher 1980: "I'll tell you a funny story about that inning and the dogs. There was actually a horse in the bullpen in the ninth inning! The cops had their dogs all around the field. The fans were screaming louder than I ever heard in my life. So I'm watching all this like I'm one of the fans. And suddenly, after that famous pop-up, Dallas Green calls down to the bullpen and tells me to get up and warm up. Hell, I wanted to see the game. This was real drama! So I didn't warm up. I just went back and stood by the edge of the bullpen door. Our BP Coach, Irish Mike Ryan yells at me, 'Dickie, get back up and toss! You've gotta keep throwing!' I yelled back at him, 'Yeah, right. Like Dallas is really gonna take Tug McGraw out and put me in this game!' Irish Mike got mad, but only for a second. Then he laughed and shouted, 'You've got a good point there!' When Tug got that strikeout, I was off and running into the infield. It was the greatest feeling in my life!"

MIKE SCHMIDT: "Those dogs! Man, they were everywhere! Big dogs! When Tug was out there, all I could think was, *Please don't hit a pop-up over this way!* Actually, that was only one of the thoughts running through my mind. The other was what I was gonna do when we won the game. On the way to the park that day, I had said to Tug, 'Hey, if you're on the mound when we win, I want to get into that photo!' That was sort of a joke because Tug had a running gag with the starting pitchers. He'd go up to Dick Ruthven or LC [Larry Christenson] before the game and ask them innocently, 'Are you pitching tonight?' When they said yes, he'd hop away shouting, 'Great, then so am I!' Actually, that gag seldom worked by 1980. By then, everyone knew the punch line. Anyway, I told Tug they'd put the celebration on the cover of *Sports Illustrated*. Now, I was mostly kidding about all that. But Tug remembered. After he struck Wilson out, he jumped up—as every Philadelphia fan knows—and then turned around to me. I was headed his way at full speed and dived on to him. And, sure enough, we made the cover!"

Minutes after the final out, Pennsylvania governor Dick Thornberg declared October 22, 1980—the day after the win—as Philadelphia Phillies Day throughout the state. Thousands upon thousands lined Broad Street. They took off from work, celebrated, laughed, cried, and finally, at long last, faced the winter knowing that for the first time ever, they did not have to "wait till next year."

For the city, the celebration was an all-day affair. For many super-fans, it became an extended affair capped off a few months later by the Philadelphia Eagles' first-ever Super Bowl appearance. That euphoria, unfortunately, died a premature death.

At the all-day Phillies celebration Tug McGraw, ever a spark for any nearby kindling, snagged as many headlines in his former stomping grounds in the Big Apple as he did in Philly. Tug announced, "All through baseball history, Philadelphia has had to take a back seat to New York City. Well, New York City can take this world championship and stick it! 'Cause we're number one!"

By the 2000 reunion, a more mellow Tug had rethought, or more accurately, thought through the statement.

McGRAW: "People sometimes say things in the moment, things that don't quite reflect what you really feel. When I made that statement, I guess it was a little bit of a good-natured dig at New York, but really, mostly, I said it just to pump up Philadelphia. Philly's a great city that never gets its due. I wanted to make sure Philly got its due for a change. Maybe I went a little overboard."

Amidst all the ballyhoo, bacchanalia, and well-worn tales of the Phils' first world championship at the '80 Phils reunion, I had my most memo-rable conversation with Ramon Aviles, an unassuming 28-year-old utility man on the 1980 squad. Ramon was no star, simply one of the mere mortals who struts and frets his hour on the stag, and then is heard no more. Ramon's major-league career lasted just one more season

RAMON AVILES: "When I was a kid, I used to see the World Series on TV in Puerto Rico. I used to see the teams celebrate and think some-thing like that could never happen to me. I could hope for it, but magical things like that could never happen to me. When Tug got the last out that nigh, and we all ran on to the field, it was amazing. It didn't matter whether you were a big star like Tug or Schmitty or Lefty, or whether you were a nobody like me! Everybody was equal. We all won the champion-ship together. And even all those wonderful people in the stands our fan —they were part of this championship, too.

"When a million people came out for the parade the next day and gave us all those warm cheers and expressions of love, I couldn't believe I was living that magic I used to watch on TV as a kid. I was living a dream that so many other wonderful people never get to experience. I was so happy inside because I knew that with the money I would get from the World Series, I would be able to buy my mother a house in Puerto Rico. And that's what I did. And how blessed I was to be part of it all!"

chapter 9

Wheeze

There's scant coverage of the 1983 NL pennant-winning Phillies in Philadelphia. In a city starved for success, a city that idolizes its athletes, a city that, like rock 'n' roll, never forgets, the 1983 Wheeze Kids have been effaced to a surprising extent from Philly lore. I can understand why Yankees fans might forget or undervalue one of their 40 teams that played in the World Series. But the Phils have only had a handful. Oops! The Phils have had six. I forgot the 1983 team. See what I mean?

I posed that question in one of my sports columns a few years back. The answers siloed into three categories: (1) The '83 Phillies weren't really *Phillies*. They were contractors; (2) The '83 Phils weren't good or exciting; (3) The '83 Phils were an embarrassment in the World Series.

The '83 roster swarmed with recognizable names. Unfortunately, they were recognizable for glory wearing other uniforms. The '83 Phils were capable of fielding 3/8 of the Big Red Machine's starting position players: 41-year-old Tony Perez, 39-year-old Joe Morgan, and 42-year-old Pete Rose. Perez and Morgan are Hall of Famers. As for Rose, well, you're a baseball fan, you know the story. The batting averages of that trio were .241, .230, and .245, respectively—hardly the stuff of the Big Red Machine's glory days.

Morgan and Perez were in Philly for one year only. Hence the "they were contractors" charge. Morgan came to the Phils along with Al Holland in a December '82 trade that sent Mike Krukow, Mark Davis, and Charles Penigar to the Giants. Little Joe was released less than a year later on Halloween—15 days after the final game of the 1983 World Series.

The *real* Phillies—the ones the fans had cheered and booed and raised a hullabaloo for—were guys like Mike Schmidt, Steve Carlton,

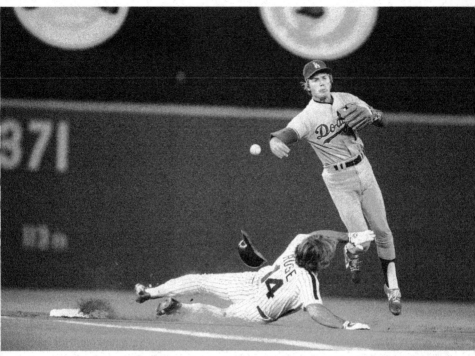

Pete Rose (14) slides into second base to break up a double play attempt by the Dodgers' Steve Sax, who made a late throw to first base, during the third inning of Game 4 of the NLCS on Saturday, October 8, 1983, in Philadelphia. *(AP Photo/Ray Stubblebine)*

Bull Luzinski, Larry Bowa, Bake McBride, Bob Boone, Garry Maddox, and Manny Trillo. By '83 only Schmidt and Carlton remained. Schmidt wasn't at his finest in '83. He hit just .255 and struck out a league-leading 148 times. But he also slammed 40 home runs—the third and final time he ever reached 40 in a season. Garry Maddox's .275 batting average led all regulars. With the exception of Von Hayes (.265), every '83 starter batted less than .260. Carlton won 15 but lost 16. Longtime Phillies hurlers Larry Christenson, Dick Ruthven, and Marty Bystrom all had losing records. John Denny, who had only joined the Phils the previous September, hurled a Cy Young season. His record was a glittery 19–6.

However, Big John left Philadelphia for Cincinnati after only three-plus years of wearing a Phillies uniform. Removing his '83 stats from his composite record as a Phillie, he was an 18–23 pitcher as a Phil. That's the charges that the 1983 Phils were contractors.

In the '83 World Series opener, Jim Dwyer tagged John Denny for a first-inning round-tripper. But Joe Morgan and Garry Maddox each answered with solo shots that gave the Phils a 2–1 victory and a 1–0 Series advantage.

Essentially, that was the World Series for the Phils. They dropped four straight contests after the opener. Most were dull affairs devoid of heroics and heroes. In the five-game Series, the Phils scored nine runs and batted .191. No one was more futile than Schmidt, who managed a lone hit in 20 at-bats.

The lifeless Series followed a lifeless season. As late as August 29, the Phils were only one game above .500 (64–63). Remarkably in this strange season, that mark was good enough for second place. From mid-September until the finale, the Phils were on fire. Starting September 16, they ran off 11 straight wins, and they won 14 of the final 16 games of the season. On the strength of that surge, they swept away five months of mediocrity, secured a comfortable lead, took the division title, and went on to grab the NL flag. But their half-month rush was too short and too late to ignite a fan base that remained loyal to their beloved departed seventies-era Phils and ambivalent toward an unfamiliar cobbled-together cast associated with rival and enemy squads.

Mr. T

The biggest contributor among the contractors on the '83 squad was the man they called "Mr. T," Al Holland. Mr. T spent only two years in Philly, 1983 and 1984. His '83 performance won him both *The Sporting News* NL Fireman of the Year Award and Rolaids Relief Man of the Year Award. Unquestionably, Holland put up impressive numbers during that pennant-winning season—100 Ks in 91.2 innings, an 8–4 record, a 2.26 ERA, and 25 saves. He placed sixth in Cy Young Award voting and ninth in the MVP tally. His numbers notched down in '84 but not enough to deny him his first and only All-Star squad selection. Nonetheless, the following year, only a few days into the '85 season, Mr. T was headed to the Pirates for reliever Kent Tekulve.

Mr. T's '85 odyssey wasn't over. In August he was traded to the California Angels, where he was 0–1 with a 1.48 ERA. In his 24.1 innings of work as an Angel, he surrendered only four runs. Unfortunately, all four left the ballpark.

In November of the same year, Mr. T was granted free agency by the Angels. The Yankees picked him up. But he was out of MLB by 1987. Not surprisingly, his fondest memories are from Philadelphia where he enjoyed his greatest success and pitched in his only World Series.

MR. T: "I loved Philly. People around the country don't realize what a beautiful city it is. They don't know how great Philly folks are, either. They're generous, down to earth, and they love their Phillies. I should qualify that—they love you as long as you bring it all to the ballpark every night. Fans here know the game of baseball. You can't fool them. If you don't play this game right, they know it, and they *do not like it.* And they let you know about it—real quick, too. Every ballplayer in baseball knows that about Philly fans. It makes some guys afraid to come here. They don't want any part of the pressure. Other guys love the electricity in the park every night. They love playing in front of a noisy, rabid crowd. That's how Philly got all those guys from the Big Red Machine. They were at the end of their careers. They didn't have their old skills, but they knew how to win. And they had been through it all before, so they knew how to turn it up a few notches when crunch time came. You check out the Pirates' numbers that year. They were the team we beat out for the division title. [In 1983, the NL consisted of an East Division and a West Division. The winners of each went head-to-head for the pennant.] If you looked at numbers alone, you'd think the Pirates won. But numbers don't win. It takes commitment and heart, and the '83 Phillie team had lots of both."

At first glance, Mr. T is right. The Pirates—at least statistically—were glitzier if not superior. Three Pirate regulars batted better than .300:

Pitcher Tug McGraw embraces teammate Al Holland after Holland pitched the final inning in the Phillies' 7–2 win over the Dodgers for the NL championship on Saturday, October 8, 1983, in Philadelphia. *(AP Photo/Ray Stubblebine)*

catcher Tony Peña (.301), third baseman Bill Madlock (.323), and left fielder Mike Easler (.307). At every position other than shortstop and center field, the Pirates' regular player had a higher average than his Phillie counterpart.

In the pitching department, the Pirates had a strong crop of starters: Rick Rhoden, Larry McWilliams, John "the Candyman" Candelaria, Lee Tunnell, and Jose DeLeon.

MR. T: "The Pirates had good starters, but I think we had the strongest 'pen in the National League. I'm not bragging, but I think that was the major reason for our success. Ron Reed and Willie Hernandez had great years [Reed was 9–1, Hernandez 8–4] and Tug [McGraw] wasn't what he once was but he contributed [Tug was 2–1, 3.56]. As for our starters, our two main horses, Lefty and Denny, kept us in most games all year long. But that's what I'm saying. We had a group of veterans who knew how to win. We didn't win pretty. But we stayed close all game and then found a way to win. Other teams couldn't match our know-how."

No one accused the '83 squad of being pretty in any sense of the word.

LARRY CHRISTENSON: "Mr. T used to joke about his 'summer teeth.' Some are here, some are there."

Christenson is referring to Mr. T's unusual asymmetrical dental layout.

LARRY CHRISTENSON: "Mr. T's teeth kind of fit his image on the mound. They made him look mean. He didn't mind that. He was an intense competitor. He was all business out there, and he'd take whatever edge he could. He went out to do a job, and he usually got it done. He didn't do things pretty, but he got it done."

MR. T: "Yeah, a lot of the guys kidded me about my teeth. Guys on that team were always on somebody about something. We had a great bunch.

"I came to Philly at kind of a strange time. Phillies fans were tied to the teams of the seventies. Those players were all homegrown. Aside from Rose, I don't know if the fans ever got around to warming up to Perez or Morgan. They were enemies for so long in Cincinnati.

"The '83 Phils were put together basically as a one-year club. As soon as the '83 season ended, Rose, Morgan, and Perez left. Ron Reed retired after the season. Willie Hernandez came to the Phils in May of '83 and was sent to Detroit after the season. Diaz and DeJesus lasted only two more years in Philly. Diaz was hurt practically the entire year, and he stayed in Philly only a couple months longer than me.

"As for 1984, with Hernandez and Reed gone, we lost our setup men. Those guys were essential, and they made my job easier as the closer.

"But, as I said, Phillies fans are sharp. They pretty much knew that a big chunk of the '83 squad, including me, wasn't going to be in town very long, so the fans never felt the same kinship for the '83 team as they did for the teams that played before us. That's understandable. Speaking personally, the Philly fans treated me great. Philly and San Francisco were my favorite cities. I grew up in North Carolina. That's where I live now. It's my home. But I could easily live in Philly or San Francisco, too."

What was the secret of Mr. T's 1983 success?

MR. T: "I can't really say. I didn't pitch any different. Everybody basically knew what they were going to get when they faced me. I was going to come right at them with fastballs. I had a breaking ball, too. But the fastball was my No. 1 pitch. I figured if somebody's going to beat me, they're going to beat me on my best pitch. I never wanted to second-guess myself after a game. I threw a two-seam fastball and a four-seamer pretty much exclusively. But I always pitched with a closer's mentality. I figured I could challenge anybody because I didn't think anybody could beat me."

And where did the Mr. T tag come from?

MR. T: "That's the question I get asked most often. Well, there's no funny backstory on that one, no drama. One of our '83 pitchers, Ed Farmer, gave the Mr. T name to me one day as I was walking up the runway headed back to the clubhouse after winning a game. Ed shouted, 'Here comes Mr. T!' It wasn't so much about my personality. It was because I wore a gold chain around my neck. A lot of guys today wear them. But in those days, it was more unusual, I think. I only wore those two necklaces because my wife gave them to me. That's all there was to it. But a bunch of reporters heard the 'Mr. T' and they ran with it. They said that's the nickname my teammates called me. It wasn't. But once they started the ball rolling, Mr. T became my nickname. I didn't mind. I liked it. I thought it fit."

Fired

Pat Corrales has made his mark in the annals of MLB managers. In the long history of the game, Corrales was only the fourth guy to manage in both leagues in the same season. He's also the first major league manager of Mexican-American descent. But his most memorable albeit dubious achievement is that he's the only manager ever fired from a first-place team. He earned that distinction when the Phils deposed him as their skipper on July 17, 1983.

Intuition suggests that would be an exclusive club.

When Corrales was sacked on July 17, 1983, the Phils were indeed in first place. Barely. The 43–42 [.50588] Phils staked that first-place claim by virtue of a .00027 advantage over the second-place 45–44 [.50561] St. Louis Cardinals.

Two days and two losses later, with Paul Owens, Corrales' replacement, at the helm, the Phils had tumbled down to third place.

Corrales made his major league playing debut as a Phillie in the ominous year of 1964.

JOHNNY CALLISON: "I remember Pat when he broke in. He showed up sometime in August of '64 when things were going our way and we were headed for a pennant. He didn't play much in '64, but he saw a fair amount of playing time in '65.

"Pat was quiet. Of course, he was a rookie when I knew him, and rookies in those days kept their mouths shut. He used to hang around with Ruben Amaro who grew up in Mexico. Pat was a Mexican who grew up in California like me. He was a young hopeful back then. He was only with us for two years, but I could tell early on that he was a student of the game. First of all, he was a catcher. They tend to analyze the game more than guys at other positions. Most position players obsess about their swings, and that's all! I know I did.

"Pat was a crafty guy. I can give you an example of how crafty. He figured out how to get on base through catcher's interference! He got on base a lot that way. Mauch loved that. Mauch loved guys who took every little advantage they could, legal or otherwise.

"Anyway, at the tail end of the '65 season, Pat did something I never saw before or since. We played the Cubs and they were trying out a young catcher. I don't remember the guy's name. Pat wasn't a talented hitter. He was struggling to hang on in the majors. He was a good defensive catcher, but he didn't hit. Anyway, Pat managed to 'steal' first base twice in one game on catcher's interference. Mauch was delighted. The Cubs' manager, a southern guy named Lou Klein, really squawked. Neither Klein nor the catcher lasted long in the majors. Corrales managed to stretch his career out. He lasted a long time for the talent he had."

No matter how many times Corrales, or "Ike" as he was nicknamed, stole first on catcher's interference, he couldn't compensate for a lifetime .216 BA. He stayed in the majors as a player until 1973 and he re-emerged in 1978 as the 37-year-old manager of the Texas Rangers. Corrales kept that job until 1980 before Don Zimmer replaced him.

Corrales was unemployed during the strike-ravaged '81 season. When Phils' manager Dallas Green left for an enhanced front-office position in the Windy City, the Phils hired him. Corrales inherited a Phillies team that was a mere vestige of the team that had won the 1980 World Championship. Among position players, only Mike Schmidt remained. Schmidt was at his peak. But Steve Carlton, age 37, was not the dominant stopper of his prime. Dick Ruthven, with an 11–11 season, was teetering toward decline. Ruthven was shipped off to Chicago ingloriously the following year ('83) after getting off to a horrendous 1–3, 5.61 start. The darling of the Philly fans, Tug McGraw was a shell of his former self. Still, carried by Carlton's Cy Young year and a productive year from Schmidt, the '82 Phils contended. Their 89–73 mark was the finest Corrales had ever achieved and would ever achieve in 10 years of managing at the professional level.

BILL GILES: "That '83 season, with Pat Corrales, was a tough year for everybody. We had so many new faces on the team. The fans fell in love with the guys on the seventies Phillies, and they were a bit confused by all the new faces.

"But with the professionalism and experience we brought in, like Joe Morgan and Tony Perez, despite their age, the organization had confidence all season that we could prevail. We had a tough bullpen and solid pitching, and our veterans knew how to compete. And every one of those veterans wanted one more World Series ring. The team just stalled for so long that year under Pat. Of course, the whole rest of the division was stalled. But we believed a change in manager might shake things up and unstall the team."

So on July 18, 1983, Pat Corrales was fired from his first-place team. The official reason was that the Phillies "were not playing up to their potential." Paul "the Pope" Owens, a longtime Phillie functionary, replaced Corrales.

The 43–42 Phils played at a 47–30 clip under their new skipper. In retrospect, was Owens' appearance the cause of the improvement?

GARY "SARGE" MATTHEWS: "Who's to say? The guys on that team were professionals. All a manager had to do was let us play. The guys on that squad didn't particularly care for Corrales, but our team was capable of getting hot in a pennant race no matter who the manager was.

"As for the getting rid of a first-place manager, I've seen lots of stranger stuff in baseball. But with the quality of veterans on that team, I believe we would have turned that season around no matter what."

Thirteen days after leaving the Phillies, Corrales replaced Mike Ferraro as Indians manager. He spent the next four seasons in Cleveland. The Indians never achieved a higher finish than fifth during his tenure. Corrales found himself in the national sport spotlight one other time that year when he charged Oakland pitcher Dave Stewart and tried to kick him. Instead, Corrales landed ingloriously on the ground, quickly decked by a Stewart right to the jaw.

During the '87 All-Star break, Corrales was fired. The Indians at the time were en route to their second 100-loss season in three years. Since he left Cleveland, Pat has enjoyed a long career filling the undefined, ill-defined position of bench coach, one of MLB's latter-day connivances—one that would quickly be whacked off or laughed off any other business organization chart as redundant. After several years serving as Bobby Cox's bench coach in Atlanta, Pat moved on to the Washington

Nationals, and then the Los Angeles Dodgers, where he serves as a special assistant to the general manager.

Plundered

The Phils have a long tradition of—as many Phillies fans might call it—aiding and abetting the Cubs. To a Phillies fan, the mere mention of the name Ryne Sandberg or Ferguson Jenkins is like waving a red flag in front of a bull. Sadly, most current fans think the Cubs took more Philadelphia treasure than the Vikings plundered from all of England in their heyday. Those same Phillies fans would finger April 21, 1966, as the start of Cubs plundering. That's the date that the Phils dished off Ferguson Jenkins, along with Adolfo Phillips (who was the main guy in the deal at the time), and John Herrnstein to the Cubs in return for a pair of twilight-of-their-career hurlers, Bob Buhl and Larry Jackson.

Those fans would be wrong. Phillie beneficence toward the Cubs started long before that disastrous giveaway. Way back on December 11, 1917, Philadelphia endowed the Cubs with their franchise player, Grover Cleveland Alexander. Bill Kellefer was a throw-in with Alexander. In exchange, the Cubs parted with the legendary Pickles Dillhoefer and Mike Prendergast plus $55,000, or as current Phillies fans might like to think of it, about 60–70 percent of what Cole Hamels will earn in 2014 for pitching a single inning. True, $55,000 in 1917 went a lot further when Pete Alexander was drinking in Philly bars and dealing on Philly mounds.

Grover Cleveland Alexander won 190 games as a Phil. He strung together three 30-win seasons from 1915 through 1917. He led the NL each of those years in strikeouts. In 1915 and 1916, he also had the league's lowest ERA. He won two pitching triple crowns during that stretch. He led the Senior Circuit in shutouts all three years, with a mind-boggling 16 shutouts in 1916 alone. To make that relevant to current fans, Alexander's shutout total was just one less than Cole Hamels' 2012 entire win total.

Apparently 1917 Phils management saw something in William Martin "Pickles" Dillhoefer beyond his .126 BA as a Cub in 1917. Their disappointment in his performance was so great when Pickles managed only one hit in his first 11 AB's as a Phil in 1918 that they shuttled him off to St. Louis. Pickles ended his career there three years later with a .223 lifetime BA as his legacy. Pitcher Mike Prendergast, the other plum that came the Phils way in the Alexander trade, went 13–14 as a Phil the year following the deal. The next year, 1919, Prendergast's career crashed and burned for good, thanks to his 0–1, 8.40 performance.

Meanwhile, Alexander continued his Hall of Fame career in Chicago where he tacked on 128 more wins. He spent his declining years in St. Louis where he added 55 more victories, even though at that point he was pitching mainly on fumes (bourbon fumes). Alexander wound up as the third winningest pitcher in baseball history, In addition to his No. 3 ranking in all-time wins, Alexander also has the distinction of being the only ballplayer ever portrayed in film by a future President of the United States. Ronald Reagan played Grover Cleveland Alexander in the 1952 film, *The Winning Team*.

Moving from the Phillies' gifting of Grover Cleveland Alexander to the Cubs to the team's gifting of Ferguson Jenkins that took place on April 21, 1966, conventional wisdom says that the Phils exported 282 victories while importing a scant 47—six from Bob Buhl and 41 from Larry Jackson. Lost in the frustration is that those 47 victories—all of which accrued from 1966–68—eclipsed Fergie's 46 during the same stretch. Buhl, once a great pitcher, was a washout as a Phillie. He went 6–8 in 1966 and 0–0 in 1967. He hung up his spikes after that. On the other hand, Jackson's 15–13 mark in 1966 wasn't far behind staff aces Jim Bunning and Chris Short. In fact, Jackson's ERA (2.99) was significantly better than Short's 3.54. In '67, Jackson's 13 wins was second on the staff only to Bunning's 17. In 1968, Jackson's final year as a Phil, his 2.77 ERA was the best on the staff. His 13 wins were second only to Short's 19 victories.

Meanwhile in Chicago, after a 6–8 campaign in 1966, Fergie reeled off six consecutive 20-or-more-win seasons en route to the Hall of Fame. His 20–12 season in 1972 would certainly have complemented Steve Carlton's amazing 27 wins that year.

Chicago Cubs second baseman and former Philadelphia Phillie Ryne Sandberg waits for the throw, and the Phillies' Von Hayes dives for the bag, attempting to steal second during the third inning in Chicago on Saturday, June 16, 1984. Hayes was called out, but Philadelphia won 8–2. *(AP Photo/ Charile Bennett)*

Moving on to 1981, Dallas Green became the main pipeliner for the Philly-to-Chicago pipeline. After the Tribune Company purchased the Cubs from the Wrigleys in 1981, the new owners lured Green away from the Phillies to become their executive vice president and general manager.

Never one to avoid provocation, Green helped initiate the slogan "Building a New Tradition." In some quarters, the slogan was perceived as a jab by Green that the Cubs' tradition was losing. As architects of that new tradition, Dallas wooed a slew of coaches and scouts away from the Phillies. Green hired Lee Elia as the Cubs' first manager. Elia had been Green's college roommate at Delaware. He brought John Vukovich over as a coach. Green also hired Gordon Goldsberry, who had been the Phillies' director of player development.

Green made a batch of trades with the Phillies, picking up Keith Moreland, Dan Larson, and Dickie Noles, among others. But those trades were trifles to Phillies fans. The trade that sticks eternally in Philly's craw was Green's timely plucking of Ryne Sandberg from the Phillies' womb.

In effect, Sandberg was a throw-in to a blockbuster shortstop swap that ticketed the Phils' Larry Bowa to the Windy City and the Cubs' Ivan DeJesus to Philly. Bowa was one of the main men in the Phils' 1970s teams as well as the 1980 World Championship team. The Bowa-DeJesus part of the deal turned out, arguably, to be a wash.

Prior to the trade, two things attracted the Phils to DeJesus. He led the NL in runs scored in 1978, and he was only 29 years old. Bowa was 36. His skills were considered to be on the decline, even though his .283 BA in 1981 (the season before the trade) was the third highest of his career. But the Phils had his decline pegged correctly. As the Cubs' starting shortstop, Bowa batted .246, .267, and .223 during the next three years. DeJesus sputtered through the next three campaigns at .239, .254, and .257.

DICKIE NOLES, Phillies pitcher in the early eighties: "Dallas outsmarted everyone in that trade. But at the time, no one could predict what a major star Ryne Sandberg would turn out to be. Lots of guys in this league have talent. What Ryne had going for him, besides natural talent, was a great work ethic. He was always an outstanding gloveman. He started winning Gold Gloves in his first or second year. But his power didn't develop 'til after I had left the Cubs. I don't think he even hit 10 home runs in his first few years when Ryne and I were teammates.

"But as I said, he worked hard, built up strength, kept himself in good shape, stayed clean, and it all paid off. He's a role model not only for kids but for his peers. More people could achieve what he did if they kept themselves clean and out of trouble and kept their focus on the game. That was Ryne's secret, and it landed him in the Hall of Fame. Simple as that."

chapter 10
Cheese Whiz

I've traveled the country fairly extensively, always with my Philly antennae up. I'm scanning what the rest of the world says about us—about our city, our teams, our schools, etc. I've found that Philly would do well to heed what poet Robert Burns admonished: "O would some power the gift give us, to see ourselves as others see us." Most people's self-image tends to be more flattering than the opinion others hold of them. In Philly's case, it's the opposite. Non-Philadelphians who have spent time there tend to view our hometown in a more favorable light than natives. On the West Coast, where many Philadelphians like Bill Cosby, Will Smith, Kevin Bacon, Sly Stallone, Bradley Cooper, Terrence Howard, etc., have migrated, I've met many people who praise Philly with phrases like, "Philadelphia is the best kept secret in the country," "Philly's an amazing place," "I never knew how terrific that city was until I lived there in college," and "I worked in Philly for a couple of years—what a great place!"

The point is that no one seems to diss Philadelphians more than Philadelphians. I have to admit, I've watched that situation improve. Philadelphia is *not* the same city it was in the fifties and sixties when it was deteriorating, soulless, and rudderless. Philly is no longer the city where the sidewalks roll up at 9:00 PM, where Blue Laws strangle and mangle nightlife, where restaurants are inferior, and where urban decay is galloping.

What turned Philly around? What spurred the uptick in image? The answer is a number of things. In the seventies, the nation's bicentennial and Philly's restaurant revolution gave the city some long-absent culinary credentials. Gentrification of many historic city neighborhoods—Queen's Village, Penn's Landing, Fairmount, Northern Liberties, and others—helped beautify and recapture the original grace of colonial and neighborhood charm. The Constitution Center that debuted in 2003 gave us a national hub—a lightning rod to draw world-class political figures and a centerpiece for our unparalleled historic district. And our sport scene played a significant role as well. We have dynamite new stadiums, an attractive sports zone in South Philly and, after decades of second-class status, several Philadelphia franchises have become consistent contenders. And occupying a prominent spot somewhere within the mixed bag of reasons for Philly's re-ascendance is a scruffy band of baseball players readily identifiable by the beards, bellies, and biceps that comprised the 1993 Phils. The '93 squad commanded more attention than any other Philadelphia team had ever enjoyed. They remain one of Philly's greatest sport legacies.

Ambassadors

"They're sloppy, grubby, and they're always stuffing their faces with something," wrote Mike Downey of the *L.A. Times.* "They should be called 'The Cheese Whiz Kids.'"

The 1993 Phils gathered a bunch of different nicknames as they rolled merrily along through the season that longtime Quaker City sportswriter Bill Lyon called "The Enchanted Season." They were dubbed at sundry times, "The Beards, Bellies, and Biceps," "The Scruffies," "The Merry Kruksters," "The Cheese Whiz Kids," "The Macho Row-sters," and "Gypsies, Tramps, and Thieves." There was also a handful of less salubrious sobriquets I won't list.

Nicknames notwithstanding, the '93 Phils won the franchise's first pennant since 1983—engineering an amazing worst-to-first flip-flop to do so. They finished dead last in 1992 and first in 1993. In 1993, they monopolized first place, clinging to the top spot every day of the campaign except for one day early in the season.

They did so with a team of second-tier stars, guys other teams were sure would never cash in on their potential, over-the-hill discards, pesty and testy vets, clubhouse lawyers—in short, a cabal of the disrespected and disrespectful. GM Lee Thomas cobbled together the group with significant input from manager Jim Fregosi and a nucleus of players led by catcher Darren Daulton.

MITCH WILLIAMS: "Jim Fregosi went out and got a prison squad. I never saw a manager get so much out of a group of players. No other manager could have managed that team. We didn't have any of the premier guys in the league—at least no one that the rest of baseball recognized as marquee players. But we had guys who would do anything to win. Some of us were just, let's just say, a bit of a challenge to manage. Fregosi knew how to handle us. We looked like a bunch of gypsies, tramps, and thieves. But Fregosi didn't hassle us about how we looked. He didn't care. He knew he could never question anyone on that team about not trying. And he never did. He let us play and just be ourselves. That was the reason for that team's success."

The '93 Phils made the nation stand up and notice. It wasn't just their look. It was their aggressive, Katy-bar-the-door style of play. They brought a hard-work blue-collar ethic to the field that the Philly fans absolutely sucked up. They were gritty, dirty-uniformed guys who looked more like an industrial-league team than a bunch of high-paid pro athletes. Of course, even calling them athletes would get under the craw of a guy like John Kruk. In one ballyhooed incident, a woman saw Kruk smoking a cigarette. She started to berate him about how horrible it was for kids to see "an athlete" smoking and what a terrible example he was setting. Kruk's famous or infamous retort (famous enough to be used as the title of his book) was, "I ain't no athlete, lady. I'm a ballplayer."

Kruk was the poster child for the unkempt scruffiness of the Beards, Bellies, and Biceps crew.

KRUK: "It didn't matter what we looked like. We went out to the diamond every day with only one thing in mind—to beat the hell out of whoever was in front of us. They tell me modern ballplayers don't play the game like that. I can't speak for every other team, but I do know I was never with a group of ballplayers as focused on winning as the '93 Phils.

First baseman John Kruk is struck out in the third inning by Atlanta Braves pitcher John Smoltz for the second time in Game 4 of the NLCS on Sunday, October 10, 1993, in Atlanta. *(AP Photo/Rusty Kennedy)*

I played for San Diego, and their clubhouse was nothing like the Phils'. So if our approach means the '93 Phils played the game the way the old timers played it, then yes, we were throwbacks. Hell, we were throwbacks no matter how you slice it. We were throwbacks because other organizations threw us back like you throw fish back in the pond because they ain't good enough to keep."

As the '93 season wore on, the Phils attracted more and more national attention. Their look, their demeanor, and their all-out Gashouse Gang style of play kept them centerstage. With each national Phillies broadcast and each national media and magazine story, the nation fell more and more under the charm of Philly's unlikely band of gypsies, tramps, and thieves. But Philadelphia also benefited. Media coverage also included images of Philadelphia's sleek, modern skyline. Beautiful vistas of the Parkway, Boathouse Row, and the Liberty Bell Mall were swept into the national consciousness. For the first time, Philly had cachet, baby!

ED RENDELL, former Philadelphia mayor and Pennsylvania governor: "Philadelphia certainly has grown into a city with attitude. In terms of civic pride, we're leaps and bounds beyond what we were several decades ago. A lot of cities claim they're unique. Maybe they are, maybe they're not. But Philadelphia *is* unique, and I can actually put the reason why into words.

"Philadelphia has a rare split personality. On the one hand, Philly has one of the biggest, broad-shouldered, working-class communities in the nation. But on the other hand, Philly contains one of the most respected art communities in the country. Our art scene is amazing. We have world-class museums and renowned art schools. We have more statues in Fairmount Park than there are in any other city park in the country. We have the Franklin Institute, the National Constitution Center, ethnic museums, the Mummers, and the Mummers Museum. And, unquestionably, we have the finest historical sites in the country.

"Then there's our sports scene with some of the most loyal, rabid fans in the country. We have a beautiful sports complex concentrated in

South Philly. So when you throw all these different influences together, you come up with something complex and unique—Philadelphia.

"Philadelphians are finally coming to realize, I think, what a great city we live in. We didn't have nearly as much city pride when I took over as mayor in the early nineties. One of my biggest goals was to put Philly on the map—to make it a place people want to come to visit, stay, and sightsee. I really give kudos to that '93 team for helping to push that agenda along. A big hurdle was trying to change the image of the city. Philly was always stymied by its image as a stodgy, boring place where there was nothing to see or do. I wanted to showcase Philly as a fun place—I wanted to convince vacationers and visitors that they'd have lots of fun in Philly. I couldn't have been luckier than to have that '93 Phillies team come along when they did, perfectly timed with our efforts to sell Philly as a fun place. These guys looked like they were having fun every second they were on the field; and for the first time, with the eyes of the whole nation on the Phils, the message about Philly being fun got conflated, which I always felt significantly helped change the city's image.

"The '93 Phils appeared in so many games of the week. They were featured in so many national magazines. They were shown so often on ESPN. Their timing was great. I loved that team, and I love what they did for the Philadelphia image! If I tried, I couldn't have hired a better group of ambassadors for Philadelphia."

The Beards, Bellies, and Biceps crew drew crowds like no other team in Philly history. They topped the three million mark for the first time in the club's (to that point) 119-year history. Attendance in 1993 topped the Quaker City's next-best year in attendance by 300,000 spectators—and I'm speaking here of *Quaker City* attendance, including years that Philadelphia had two major league franchises.

JIM FREGOSI, 1993 Phillies manager: "People come up to me yet and ask how we managed to corral all those characters on one team. We looked for chemistry, I'll admit. Lee Thomas, our GM, really believed in chemistry. We had a lot of veterans on that team who had never made it to the postseason. For a lot of them, it was now or never. They played that way every game—like there was no tomorrow.

"Maybe we did go after the crazy guys. I always liked the zany types. I think they make the game interesting, fun for the fan. With the nucleus we had from '92, we figured we could bring those zany types into the locker room and it would all work. I didn't decide that on my own. I asked the vets their opinions before we went after people to bring in."

DARREN "DUTCH" DAULTON, catcher and 1993 Phillies team captain: "Fregosi was amazing the way he included the players in building that team. He told us we were not going to win on 'star power.' We needed guys who played the game hard and smart. He needed to solicit our opinions on opponents. He said he was looking for players who played with heart. He called all the vets together—Mitch Williams, the Dude [Lenny Dykstra], Mickey Morandini, Head [Dave Hollins], and Terry Mulholland—and we talked about what guys we could bring in that would feed into that kind of attitude. That's how we got Inky [Pete Incaviglia]. Fregosi mentioned his name as a prospect and, right around the table, we said, 'Go get him!' Well, no matter what kind of success we would have had, we put together a group of players who were a perfect fit for this city."

CURT SCHILLING, Phillies pitcher: "You don't shortchange Philly fans. You don't fool them. Every town claims to have intelligent fans, informed fans, and the like. But in Philly and a few other eastern cities like Boston, New York, and Baltimore, fans really are better students of the game. They have the pride and tradition that newer franchises haven't built yet because their fan bases don't go back for generations like they do in those old eastern cities. In Philadelphia, fathers raise their kids to be Phillies fans, just like their own fathers raised them to be Phillies fans, and their fathers before them. Kids are born Phillies fans. But what's most important is that they stay Phillie fans for life, even after they've moved away from the Delaware Valley. I run into Phillies fans in every town I go. Even though they're living some place else, they're totally into the Phils because of the long tradition they grew up in. It's that intensity

Starter Curt Schilling delivers a pitch against the Atlanta Braves in the opening game of the NLCS at Veterans Stadium in Philadelphia on Wednesday, October 6, 1993. Schilling struck out five in the first two innings to set an NLCS record. *(AP Photo/Rusty Kennedy)*

in Philly that I love—that some ballplayers love. Others don't, but our whole '93 squad loved it. That's who management targeted in building the team. Ballplayers either love that intensity, or hate it. In '93, our clubhouse was full of crazies who loved Philly's intensity, and fans loved us. It was a season-long love affair. And the rest of the nation picked up the vibe and ran with it. That team did a lot to put Philadelphia on the map with the rest of the country."

BILL GILES: "I still look back on that team as the most special team we ever had around here. It was the only time I ever got a call from George Steinbrenner. Ever! He called me one day out of the blue and said, 'That's really an exciting team you have down there! I'd love to have them up here in New York!'"

L-O-O-O-N-G

The longest day at the park in the history of MLB turned out to be July 2, 1993. In fact, forget your "most unbeatable MLB record" list— Cy Young's 511 wins, Connie Mack's 3,731 wins as a manager, and Joe DiMaggio's 56-game hit streak. No day of baseball, other than July 2, 1993 has ever finished at 4:40 AM the following day. It was truly the longest day, and true to form for the '93 squad, the "day" finished unconventionally.

TOM BURGOYNE, Phillie Phanatic: "I remember how July 2 began for me. I used to travel around to the Philly radio stations in those days and give away Phillies merchandise and tickets and the like for promotions. It was a great job, and the DJs sure loved the free stuff. You can't beat 'free.'

"After my last stop, I drove by Independence Hall and saw they were taping *The Today Show*. There were TV lights and huge TV trucks everywhere on the lawn at Independence Hall. I could see Bryant Gumbel and Sara James lounging on director's chairs on a platform behind the pavilion where the Liberty Bell is displayed.

"My 'Phanatic Sense' was tingling. How could the Phanatic pass up a chance at national TV? I double-parked next to a production truck, zipped into the back of the van, and presto! Just like Clark Kent, I suited up and beelined toward the cameras. As I hopped out, I saw Mayor Rendell chatting with Bryant about 50 yards away. I grabbed two Phillies caps, rushed over and gave them each one. Peter Nero and the Philly Pops were seated nearby, so I started 'conducting' them. The producer, Biff Henderson, who I knew from a visit on *Late Night with David Letterman*, came running over waving his arms, 'Hey, whatcha doin' here? We're shooting a live show. You gotta beat it!' But his wry smile tipped me off that something else was afoot. I turned around, and there was a smiling Bryant Gumbel headed my way. He was on the air.

"'Somebody just arrived who always makes me laugh. He's over here with the Philly Pops. Maybe we can coax him over. Hey Phanatic, c'mon and join us over here,' Gumbel insisted.

"I waddled over and did a five-minute interview, which is difficult for the Phanatic since he can't talk. I mimed my answers to questions about the Phanatic's 'love affair' with Lasorda, about whether the Cardinals would catch the Phils, and other questions. When I tried to get up to leave, my butt was wedged in the director's chair. Perhaps the audience thought I was doing some pantomime. But I wasn't. I was struggling to pry myself out of the chair. I was on the chair way longer than I was supposed to be. I wound up having more airtime than the Mayor, which is fine. I'm so much better looking. Still, I never would have believed that I wouldn't be leaving the park until the next morning a little before sunrise."

On July 2, the Phils were scheduled for a doubleheader. They had just returned from a disastrous 2–5 road trip that terminated with 9–3 and 14–5 embarrassments at the hands of the Cards. On the trip, the Phils saw their 9½-game lead whittled down to 5½.

LARRY ANDERSEN, relief pitcher for the 1993 Phillies: "Fans don't know, but our 'day' was even longer. Dutch Daulton called a team meeting beforehand. He kind of scolded us for hanging our heads against St. Louis. The Dude Dykstra chimed in, saying we weren't playing with the same swagger. Schilling, who had been shelled in the 14–5 game said,

'I embarrassed myself yesterday, and I really embarrassed the team. That'll never happen again. We gotta shake that road trip off and pick up from where we were before.' I told everybody that we pitchers were letting the hitters get too comfortable. We had to start intimidating people again. It was the most significant meeting of the season."

A betting man would have bet the house on the Phillies that game. It seemed like all the stars were aligned and the team's resolve was reaffirmed. Besides, they were back home again in front of their adoring crowd. And Terry Mulholland was on the mound. Mulholland had led the NL in stopping losing streaks the previous year when he righted the Phils' ship a dozen times. Unfortunately, he didn't have the same magic this time around, and in a soggy, dreary, rain-delayed affair, the Phils were downed 5–2 in the opener.

There had been a 2-hour, 48-minute rain delay after the fifth inning. The game resumed at 11:54 PM. Six minutes later, longtime stadium organist Paul Richardson (who has since passed away), played 12 chimes and the fan in the stands applauded. I kid. Actually, several diehards were still hanging around. They all applauded. This, after all, is Philadelphia.

At 1:03 AM, the first game ended. Shortly afterward, Dan Baker's announcement rang out across the stadium: "Game 2 will start in 20 minutes." An incredulous Richie Ashburn joked with broadcasting partner Harry Kalas, "Harry, I'm expecting you to call a great game tonight. This is the shank of the evening for you. You're usually just getting started about this hour."

In the second game, the Phils dropped behind Andy Benes 5–0 by the top of the third. Since Benes at the time had the lowest ERA in the NL, things did not augur well for the home team.

JIM EISENREICH: "Well, I never doubted we'd win. Our guys were used to watching the sun come up. The way I figured it, if they hadn't been out here at the ball park, they'd have been watching the sun come up somewhere else anyway."

LARRY ANDERSEN: "I was proud of our relief corps that night. We basically shut the Padres down the rest of the way after they got the five-run lead. I came into the game after 3:30 AM. I remember passing by first-base umpire Wally Bell and telling him I was usually indisposed at this hour of the evening and I wasn't sure what to expect. But I held them down."

TOMMY GREENE: "That game and that night was crazy! Can you imagine that I got into the second game as a pinch-runner? Our roster was so depleted they had to use me. What I remember most about being in the game was that when I was standing on second base, I got to see one of the best fights I ever saw out in the left-field upper deck."

A little known fact (and a sure winner in a bar bet) is that the top hitters on the '93 Phillies roster were Larry Andersen and Mitch Williams. Both batted 1.000 for the season. Both were 1-for-1. Mitch got his hit for the year that night at 4:40 AM, and he got it off one of baseball's finest closers, Trevor Hoffman. It was the game-winning, walk-off single.

MITCH WILLIAMS: "Hoffman had a wicked forkball. I didn't want any part of it. I looked back at Kevin Higgins, the Padres catcher, and said, 'I'll wrap this bat around you if you call for the forkball.' I think I started my swing while Hoffman was still looking in for the sign. I love to swing the stick, although if you don't swing it well, sometimes it's better to look lazy than bad. But this time I just swung hard—just in case I made contact."

PETE INCAVIGLIA, Phillies outfielder: "I was the one who scored that winning run when Mitch knocked it in. I'll be honest. I had mixed emotions. Sure, I was tired and it was late and I wanted to go home. But if Mitch got a hit, I knew we'd never hear the end of it. Just before he singled, he hit a foul, and when I rounded third, I told [3B coach] Bowa, 'Just watch. That little SOB is gonna get a hit, and we're never gonna hear the end of it.' Damned if he didn't and damned if we didn't."

Once

In case you've forgotten, the '93 season—the Enchanted Season—ended in a flash with one swing of the bat. Joe Carter hit a Mitch Williams pitch over the left-field fence in the sixth game of the '93 World Series

Relief pitcher Mitch Williams during Game 4 of the World Series with the
Toronto Blue Jays on October 20, 1993, in Philadelphia's Veterans Stadium.
(AP Photo/Rusty Kennedy)

as a helpless Pete Incaviglia watched in dismay. The 3,137,674 spectators who had jammed into Veterans Stadium that season felt a crippling disappointment. But as time passed, the brusque end of the season lost its sting and only the exhilaration remained at having watched one of the most diverse, wacky conglomerations of uninhibited humanity ever to prance across the American professional baseball diamond.

The team and its fans soon realized, even though it pained them to admit it—that the Beards, Bellies, and Biceps crew was a one-season phenomenon. Their field of dreams would last but one enchanted summer.

MITCH WILLIAMS: "That year was lightning in a bottle. Nobody's ever again gonna corral a group of gypsies, tramps, and thieves like we had and make it work. Hell, I can't imagine anybody else who'd ever want us! And that's the point. That's what people who don't understand the game of baseball don't get. There was power in the sheer intensity on that club. Everybody there wanted to win. We hurt when we lost. We lived and died baseball.

"There's a lot of distractions out there for baseball players. Now I'm not saying our guys didn't have their fun off the field or that they didn't squeeze everything they possibly could out of their extracurricular activities that season. But people who have never had to put a baseball uniform on for 162 days—day after day—don't know how grueling this profession can be. To walk into that clubhouse 162 times a season and then go out on the field and give everything you've got every single time you're out there—that's a tough thing to do. It's tough enough for one person to maintain that kind of intensity and focus, let alone getting 25 guys to do it. But we got 25 guys to do it.

"Yeah, that '93 team was lightning in a bottle. We fed off each other all season long. And I was totally worn down by season's end, but I never had so much fun in my life. Baseball life was never so good as it was that season. In fact, it was too good. We all loved the team so much that some of us couldn't adjust to anything different. What we had on that team sounds almost impossible to most guys who play. We were the most focused group I ever played with and yet, at the same time, we were the loosest. Whatever, once you had a taste of that atmosphere, you couldn't be happy in any other."

Williams, or "Wild Thing" as he will always be known, flew off to his ranch in Texas after delivering his ignominious pitch to Joe Carter. Williams was not aboard the team airplane that flew back to Philly after the final game of the World Series in Toronto. He would never again fly with the team as a Phillies player.

DAVE HOLLINS: "I played baseball a long time. I've been with a lot of different teams. But when I left the Phillies, I went through what I call 'Phillie withdrawal.' I'm serious. I don't know what else to call it. I never found the same atmosphere or the same desire to win with any other group. I never got the same pleasure and satisfaction playing baseball. What I'm trying to say is that my baseball life was so good and so rewarding in '93 that, in a strange way, it hurt the rest of my career. I never performed as well. I never adjusted when I was away from that atmosphere."

PETE INCAVIGLIA: "I'll second what Mitch and Head [Dave Hollins] said. I had a long career. I played with lots of different groups. I played in Texas a lot longer than I did in Philly. But when I think of myself as a ballplayer, I consider myself a '93 Phillie. Practically all the guys on the club feel that way, no matter where else they played. The team, the year, those guys, plus the fans—just everything about '93 was terrific. Put it this way—I'll always be a Phillie."

JIM FREGOSI: "It was such a special season, and we had such a special group. I've been around this game a long time, but I've never had the pleasure of being with players who devoted themselves so much to winning and who understood the ins and outs and finer points of what you need to do to win this game.

"I confess that I did think at the end of the '93 season that this was a one-year club. For one thing, the way these guys threw themselves into that season, and the way they got beat up—Dutch's bad legs, Lenny's all-out, sacrifice-your-body style—when I added everything up, well, I didn't think we could stay healthy enough to compete after '93. Besides so many of our guys were older. For better or worse, '93 was the last hurrah for them. And because of that last-ditch effort and common goal, these guys became the tightest-knit group I ever saw.

"And you know the best part of that season? The fans. The fans really understood how special these guys were. I mean, we did not win. We were the also-rans, and yet the '93 Phils are consistently picked as Philly's most beloved team. What other team loses a championship and commands that kind of devotion? Everywhere I go to this day, people come up to me and say, 'Thanks for '93!'"

Jayson Stark was a Philly writer that season—the guy closest to the team. He understood the strange chemistry that fueled this unusual group.

JAYSON STARK: "It was hard for those guys on that team to believe or accept it was over. The season was a magic-carpet ride that seemed like it would never come to an end. But of course it did.

"You have to appreciate the season for what it was because a season like that isn't normal. You can't re-create it. Whatever the formula is, you just sit back and hold it. And the players realized this season was an outlier. I ran a magazine story two days after the season. Darren Daulton and Larry Andersen were in the clubhouse to clean out their lockers. They saw Video Dan [the Phillies videographer] working on a highlight reel of the season. Dan asked them to check it out and give him their input. At that phase of production, it was just one long, unedited run. But the two of them sat there transfixed. They watched the whole season unfold again. Neither one wanted to leave. They knew that when they walked out the door, all those great moments they had just watched in Dan's video were gone. The whole season they just experienced, all those good times, were gone. What they really realized, what remained unspoken, was that those amazing times would never come back again."

Fregosi, Bill Giles, '93 Coach Denis Menke, and many of the '93 players themselves told me about how other players—rivals—around the league wanted to become Phillies themselves that year. Other players saw the rare camaraderie, the cutting up, and the freefall of fun these guys were having, and they wanted in. They saw a rare spark that was lacking in their own clubhouses. They saw wild and unfettered *joie de vivre* before games that morphed into steely, cussed resolve when those same guys got between the lines. Pittsburgh's Andy Van Slyke summed up the rest of the league's perception of the Beards, Bellies, and Biceps boys, 'People talk about how goofy the Phillies are, and to some extent, they're right. They were some goofy guys! But all you had to do is play them once to realize that these goofy guys would die for each other. They were a band of brothers. They had a lot of talented players, but I don't think that was the reason for their success. Their success started in the clubhouse.'"

During the 1993–94 winter, Mitch Williams was traded to Houston for Jeff Juden and Doug Jones. Pitcher Terry Mulholland was dealt to the Yanks. The Krukker had a battle with cancer that sidelined him for most of '94. Ruben Amaro Jr. was shuttled out to Cleveland for Heathcliff Slocumb. In midseason '94, Milt "Pops" Thompson headed to Houston, and Wes Chamberlain left for Boston. Tommy Greene, perhaps the Phils' most promising pitcher, mirrored the career of Whiz Kid precursor Bob Miller. Plagued by injuries, Tommy won just two games in '94—his final wins as a major leaguer. Ben Rivera went 3–4 in 1994 and never pitched another ML season. Larry Andersen retired after the '94 season. A chronic bad back abbreviated Lenny Dykstra's career. Dutch Daulton's leg injuries hampered his production and shortened his career.

Like the Whiz Kids and the Wheeze Kids, the Cheese Whiz Kids faded fast. After the '94 strike-mangled season, the '95 Phils finished 21 games behind division-leading Atlanta. The Cheese Whiz Kids already seemed like distant memories, eons removed. But unlike the Wheeze Kids, the '93 bunch never faded from Philly's collective memory.

The '93 lightning in a bottle was brilliant and brief. But no Phillie fan will ever forget how a wacky group of baseball players lit up a whole city for one enchanted summer.

Sources

Books

Allen, Richie, with Allen Lewis. *Richie Ashburn's Trivia*. Philadelphia, PA: Running Press, 1983.

Astor, Gerald. *The Baseball Hall of Fame 50th Anniversary Book*. Prentice Hall Press, 1988.

Clayton, Skip "Memory Lane." *Fifty Phabulous Phillies*. Champaign, IL: Sports Publishing, 2000.

Connor, Anthony J. *Voices from Cooperstown*. New York: Macmillan Publishing Company, 1982.

Coste, Chris. *33 Year Old Rookie: How I Finally Made It to the Big Leagues after Eleven Years in the Minors*. New York: Ballantine Books, 2008.

James, Bill. *The New Bill James Historical Baseball Extract*. New York: Free Press, a division of Simon & Schuster, 2003.

Jordan, David. *Occasional Glory: The History of the Philadelphia Phillies*. Jefferson, NC: McFarland & Company, 2002.

Kahn, Roger. *The Boys of Summer*. New York: Signet, 1973.

Lewis, Michael. *Moneyball*. New York: WW Norton, 2004.

Philadelphia Phillies. *Phillies Media Guide 1980*.

Philadelphia Phillies. *Phillies Media Guide 1983*.

Philadelphia Phillies. *Phillies Media Guide 1993*.

Philadelphia Phillies. *Phillies Media Guide 1999*.

Philadelphia Phillies. *Phillies Media Guide 2008*.

Philadelphia Phillies. *Phillies Media Guide 2012*.

Rogers, C. Paul. *The Whiz Kids*. Philadelphia, PA: Temple University Press, 1996.

Shannon, Mike. *Tales from the Dugout.* New York: McGraw-Hill, 1997.

Thierot, Dade. *Diary of a Phan: The Sad Summer of '94.* Woodside, CA: SouthPaw Press, 1995.

Ward, Geoffrey C., and Ken Burns. *Baseball: An Illustrated History.* New York: Alfred A. Knopf, Inc., 1994.

Westcott, Rich. *Philadelphia Phillies: Past and Present.* Minneapolis, MN: MVP Books, 2010.

Westcott, Rich. *Phillies '93: An Incredible Season.* Philadelphia. PA: Temple University Press, 1994.

Westcott, Rich. *Phillies Essential.* Chicago: Triumph Books, 2006.

Westcott, Rich, and Frank Bilovsky. *The Phillies Encyclopedia.* Philadelphia, PA: Temple University Press, 2004.

Wheeler, Chris. *View from the Booth.* Philadelphia, PA: Camino Books, 2009.

Will, George F. *Bunts.* New York: Touchstone, 1999.

Zalecki, Todd. *The Philadelphia Phillies: An Extraordinary Tradition.* Chicago: Triumph Books, 2004.

Zimniuck, Frank. *Phantastic!: The 2008 Champion Philadelphia Phillies.* Chicago: Triumph Books, 2008.

Zinn, Howard. *The People's History of the United States.* New York: First Harper Perennial Deluxe Edition, 2010.

Magazines

Sports Illustrated

Newspapers

Philadelphia Inquirer (from the Free Library of Philadelphia archives)
Philadelphia Bulletin (from the Free Library of Philadelphia archives)

Websites

Baseball-Reference.com
19 to 21, John Shiffert's webzine